The Early Irish Monastic Schools

A Study Of Ireland's Contribution To Early Medieval Culture

By

Hugh Graham

ABOUT THE AUTHOR

Hugh Graham, the writer of the masterpiece "The Early Irish Monastic Schools: A Study of Ireland's Contribution to Early Medieval Culture," is a pupil recognized for his enormous contributions to the examine of medieval Irish records and schooling. With a keen interest within the cultural history of Ireland, Graham delves into the rich history of Irish monastic colleges, offering readers a comprehensive exploration in their effect on early medieval tradition. In this influential paintings, Graham meticulously examines the position played by means of Irish monastic faculties in shaping no longer handiest the non-secular landscape but also the broader cultural and educational trends of the time. His studies shed light on Ireland's particular and precious contributions to medieval scholarship, highlighting the intellectual achievements that emanated from those monastic establishments. "The Early Irish Monastic Schools" stands as a testament to Graham's willpower to uncovering and maintaining Ireland's historical legacy. His writing skillfully combines ancient analysis with a passion for the subject, imparting readers with a profound know-how of the cultural and academic landscapes of early medieval Ireland.

CONTENTS

PREFACE

The aim of the present study is to give within reasonable limits a critical and fairly complete account of the Irish Monastic Schools which flourished prior to 900 A.D.

The period dealt with covering as it does the sixth, seventh, eighth, and ninth centuries is one of the most obscure in the history of education. In accordance with established custom writers are wont to bewail the decline of learning consequent on the Fall of the Roman Empire in the fifth century and then they pass on rapidly to the Renaissance in the fifteenth; a few, however, pause to glance at the Carolingian Revival of learning in the ninth century and to remark parenthetically that learning was preserved in Ireland and a few isolated places on the fringe of Roman Civilization, but with some notable exceptions writers as a class have failed to realise that as in other departments of human knowledge there is a continuity in the history of education. The great connecting link between the Renaissance and the Graeco-Roman culture which flourished in Western Europe during the early centuries of our era is the Irish Monastic Schools. Modern research clearly points to the conclusion that the history of these schools is in reality a chapter in the history of education in Western Europe. While we do not claim that the Irish schools were the sole factor in the preservation and transmission of letters during the Early Middle Ages we are certainly convinced that they played a leading part. The cumulative evidence which we submit amply warrants this conclusion.

The many tributes of a complimentary nature which scholars have bestowed on the work of the Irish Monastic Schools would indicate that the importance of their influence has not been overlooked; yet it seems to us that their real aim and character have not always been clearly understood. In a certain respect these schools were unique: they were neither purely classical schools of the type that flourished in Gaul in the fourth century, nor were they mere theological seminaries such as existed in certain parts of Britain and the Continent that lay outside the Irish sphere of influence. The peculiar character of the Irish monastic school would appear to be the result of the harmonious combination of three distinct elements: 1, Native Irish Culture;

2, Christianity; 3, Graeco-Roman Culture. We believe that this conception of Irish monastic culture furnishes the key to a proper understanding of the real significance of Irish scholarship during the Early Middle Ages. No study of Irish monastic schools which neglected to give due consideration to the potent influence of each of these three constituents would be adequate even if it were intelligible. The force of this conviction which is the result of a prolonged and critical examination of all the relevant material to hand has determined the form which the present study has assumed.

The first and second chapters are not merely introductory: they are fundamental. In the first chapter we discuss the question of a pre-Christian and pre-classical native Irish culture. The second chapter is devoted to an examination of that difficult problem, the beginnings of classical learning in Ireland—a matter on which modern research has thrown considerable light. As the school was so intimately connected with the monastic system it was necessary to devote a special chapter to an examination of the more salient features of Irish monasticism which differed in many ways from Continental monasticism. Here we are impressed with the fact that the native Irish ideals blended with those of Christianity so as to give the Irish monastic life a peculiarly national character which was ever reflected in the educational aims and ideals of the Irish monk even when his missionary zeal carried him far from the environment of his native land. In the fourth chapter the attempt is made to determine the precise relation which existed between the Irish monastic school and the general educational situation not only in Ireland and Britain but in Western Europe from 650 to 900 A.D. Those three great centres of intellectual life in every Irish monastery—the school room, the scriptorium and the library—are treated in the fifth chapter. The particular function of each and its relation to the others is described while their combined influence, whether of a contemporary or permanent nature, has been noticed. The all-important question of the nature of the curriculum has been critically examined in the sixth chapter. Finally, a chapter is given to a discussion of the scope of Irish scholarship and its significance in Mediæval Culture.

While a work of this nature can scarcely claim to be original and the acknowledgments are too numerous to recount, yet the grouping is new and not unfrequently facts have been presented from a new angle. Source material has been consulted where possible. The results of previous investigation have been freely used, but even as often happened when we have arrived at conclusions which have been anticipated by other writers, we have maintained quite as critical and independent an attitude as when we ventured to challenge certain popular opinions and to make such generalizations as the result of our own study seemed to warrant. In some instances, however, this study has carried us into fields of inquiry where we have no credentials, but in these cases as in every other where we have used secondary authorities acknowledgment is always made in the foot-notes.

In various ways we have endeavoured to condense a good deal of information into a limited space. For example, to avoid repetition we give frequent cross references to important topics dealt with in different parts of this study. Again, instead of attempting the bewildering and impossible task of giving an account of individual schools we have given a list of the more important ones and merely referred to particular schools as occasion demanded in order to illustrate certain points of primary importance. For similar reasons all attempts at biographical accounts of Irish scholars have been studiously avoided. Such references as have occasionally been made were necessary in carrying out our general plan which was to deal with the Irish monastic school as an educational institution. Of course it would have served no useful purpose to ignore completely those men whose acknowledged scholarship was the best testimony of the character of the instruction available in the schools in which they themselves studied and taught.

A word might be said with reference to the proportion of space occupied by the different topics. The plan invariably followed has been to give a minimum of space to any topic which is treated fairly fully elsewhere in some accessible work. On the other hand no topic which appeared to be an integral part of the general plan has been omitted and such topics as have been inadequately treated elsewhere have here received fuller consideration.

While quite conscious of the limitations of our treatment, it is hoped that by pointing out many supplementary sources of information we have done something to smooth the path of other investigators who may wish to explore those portions of the same field which lay outside the scope of our present inquiry.

The author wishes to express his sincere thanks to the following: to Dr. Fletcher H. Swift, Professor of the History of Education in the University of Minnesota, for his sympathetic interest in the subject and for his advice and guidance; to Rev. Laurence P. Murray, M.R.I.A., Principal of St. Brigid's Irish College, Omeath, Co. Louth, for the use of his excellent Irish library and for helpful suggestions and criticisms of the earlier chapters; to Rev. Dr. Peter Guilday, Professor of History in the Catholic University of Washington, D.C., for reading the MS. and for his advice and encouragement; to Mr. Patrick O'Daly of the Talbot Press for seeing the work through the press and for painstaking proof-reading; and finally to the publishers for turning out the work in an attractive and scholarly form.

COLLEGE OF ST. TERESA,
WINONA, MINNESOTA, U.S.A.,
Lá Fhéile Pádraig, 1923.

CHAPTER I
CIVILIZATION AND LEARNING IN IRELAND IN PAGAN TIMES

The precise state of civilization and learning in Ireland in pre-Christian times is difficult to determine owing to the fact that there is no native contemporary evidence of a documentary nature, while the references in the works of foreign writers are few in number and generally vague in character. Fortunately, however, there are a few sources of information which have been made available by the laborious and scholarly researches of generations of investigators. The principal of these sources are:

1. Archæology.
2. The so-called Brehon Laws.
3. Early Irish Literature.
4. Foreign Testimony.
5. Ogam Inscriptions.

A brief survey of the evidence supplied by each of these may be helpful in determining the nature and extent of Irish pagan culture.

ARCHÆOLOGICAL EVIDENCE:

Archæological research shows that Ireland was inhabited from very early times though it is impossible to fix the exact chronological limit of the earliest colonization. Passing over the beginnings of civilization which are exemplified by the crude implements and other remains of the Stone Age, we note that in the Bronze Age when the art of working metals had been discovered the existing specimens of the work of these ancient craftsmen point to a relatively advanced stage of civilization. Indeed, an examination of the discoveries of this period amply justifies the statement that "in point of wealth, artistic feeling and workmanship, the Irish craftsmen of the Bronze Age surpassed those of Britain."[1] The doyen of prehistoric chronology, Dr. Oscar Montelius of Stockholm, having studied the antiquities of the British Isles, gave the result of his labours in a memoir published in 1918.[2] This work is now the standard authority on this subject. Dr. Montelius divides the Bronze Age into five periods. In the first period he includes the Transitional

Period where copper was in use (Copper period) which he places between the middle of the third and the beginning of the second millenium, B.C. One of the greatest living Irish archæologists, Mr. George Coffey, while agreeing with the Scandinavian as to the division into five periods, would not place the first period so early as has been suggested by Dr. Montelius, but agrees that the first period ended between 2000 B.C. and 1800 B.C. Both writers would place the end of the fifth period, that is, the end of the Bronze Age about 350 B.C. Thus we may consider the Irish Bronze Age as extending approximately from 2000 B.C. to 350 B.C. Mr. Coffey in one of his valuable works gives numerous illustrations representative of each period.[3] The originals are nearly all in the National Museum, Dublin, where Mr. Coffey is the official Keeper of Irish Antiquities. A notable feature of the finds of this period is the abundance and variety of the gold ornaments. The collection of gold ornaments of Irish workmanship is the largest in the British Isles being twelve or thirteen times more than that in the British Museum.[4] Possibly, this is but a small fraction of the entire output of the Irish artists of pagan times; for many Irish gold ornaments have been discovered in Scandinavia and in Western Europe not to speak of many finds which never enter a museum.[5]

From such material remains it would appear to be a legitimate deduction that even at this early age the Irish were skilled craftsmen and acquired by some means at least an elementary and industrial and technical education and that they were already cultivating the æsthetic. Art was developing on distinctly national lines, yet the country was not isolated. There must have been direct communication with the Continent; for Mr. Coffey has traced Aegean and Scandinavian influence in the incised ornament of the New Grange group[6] and Iberian influence on some of the later type of bronze ornaments.[7]

THE BREHON LAWS:

The laws of a country dealing as they do with man in his relations to his fellow-man and society in general are always an important indication of the state of civilization attained by the race which has evolved them. In this connection a valuable source of information on the social condition and state of culture attained by the pagan Irish is the native code of laws, generally styled the Brehon Laws, but more correctly termed the *Féineachas*. According to a generally accepted tradition these laws were revised and codified in 438 A.D. by a committee of nine appointed by King Laoghaire at the suggestion of St. Patrick. The committee consisted of three kings (Laoghaire, High King of Ireland; Corc, King of Munster; and Daire, King of Cairnach); three saints (St. Patrick, himself, St. Benin and St. Cairnech);

and three learned men (Ross, Dubhthach and Feargus).[8]   These laws grew up with the people from the very beginning of society and took cognisance of them from every point of view. They professed to regulate domestic and social relations of every kind, as well as professions, trades, industries, occupations and wages.[9] As laws they are too minute; but this defect renders them valuable to the student who is interested in the social conditions of the period during which they were evolved. As a recent commentator[10] has remarked: "The rigorously authentic character of these laws relating to, and dealing with the actual realities of life and with institutions and a state of society nowhere else revealed to the same extent; the extreme antiquity both of the provisions and the language in which they were written, and the meagreness of Continental material illustrative of the same things endow them with exceptional archaic, archæological and philological interest." The development of such a comprehensive and detailed code of laws must have been the work of many generations of lawmakers and suggest a relatively high degree of native culture. In this connection one is inclined to quote the emphatic declaration of Dr. George Sigerson who has won honours both as a litterateur and as a scientist. He says: "I assert that, biologically speaking, such laws could not emanate from any race whose brains had not been subject to the quickening influence of education for many generations."[11] In other words, such a code of laws can be accounted for only on the assumption of a high degree of culture as a racial heritage of the nation which evolved them.

EVIDENCE FROM EARLY IRISH LITERATURE:

There are many passages in the oldest Irish literature, both secular and religious, which state that the Irish had books before the introduction of Christianity. In a memoir[12] of St. Patrick written in the seventh century Muirchu Maccu Machteni relates how during the contest of the saint with the druids—the learned men of the time—the High King Laoghaire proposed that one of St. Patrick's books and one belonging to the druids should be cast into the water to see which would come out uninjured—a kind of ordeal. Here it will be noticed that Muirchu's statement embodies a tradition which was old in the seventh century. The same story is told in the *Tripartite Life of St. Patrick*.[13] Both the Irish bardic tales and the oldest existing lives of St. Patrick agree in stating that he found in the country both literary and professional men—all pagans—druids, poets and antiquarians or historians,[14] as well as an elaborate code of laws.[15]

Although no Irish document has been preserved which dates earlier than the seventh century, there is ample intrinsic evidence that the earliest existing documents were copied from manuscripts which go back a century or two earlier and these again may have recorded the traditions of a still earlier period. Authorities are agreed that after the establishment of Christianity in the fifth century the Irish scholars committed to writing not only the laws, bardic historical poems, &c. of their own time, but those which had been preserved from earlier times whether traditionally or otherwise.[16] In a subsequent chapter reference will be made to a common practice of the Irish monks, namely that of making marginal and interlinear glosses on the classical writings they were studying, copying, or teaching. For the present it is sufficient to note that even in the case of the earliest of the seventh century glosses the written language was fully developed and cultivated, with a polished phraseology and an elaborate and systematic grammar having well established forms for its words and for all its rich inflections. To the linguistic student it is inconceivable how much a complete and regular system of writing could have developed in the period which had elapsed from the introduction of Christianity in the fifth century until the general spread of Christian learning in the seventh. Such a period would be much too short, especially when it is recollected that early Irish literature had its roots not in Christianity but in the native learning which was the main, and almost the sole, influence in developing it. This consideration points clearly to the conclusion that native learning was carefully and systematically cultivated before the introduction of Christianity.

Again, Irish poetry owes its development solely to the Lay Schools. [17] It had complicated prosody—with numerous technical terms[18] all derived from the Irish language. These vernacular terms used in Irish grammar contrast strikingly with the terms used to designate the offices and ceremonies of Christianity which were almost all derived from Latin. [19] All this would go to prove that Irish prosodial rules and technical terms, and of course Irish poetry itself, were fully developed before the introduction of Christianity.

FOREIGN TESTIMONY:

At least one foreign writer bears witness of the fact that the pagan Irish possessed books. A Christian philosopher of the fourth century (some would place him as early as the second or third) whose name is Aethicus of Istria wrote a Cosmography of the World in which he states that on leaving Spain he hastened to Ireland where he spent some time "examining their books" (*eorum volumina volvens*).[20] Aethicus is not by any means complimentary. He calls the Irish sages unskilled and uncultivated teachers, but he speaks of the Spaniards in a similar strain. Possibly not understanding the Irish language he regarded all learning outside of Greece and Rome as barbarous and beneath notice. However, his statement proves that when he visited

Ireland there were books at least a century before St. Patrick's advent; it also shows that he found them in such abundance that he spent some time in examining them.

OGAM INSCRIPTIONS:

The point has now been reached when it is necessary to discuss the kind of writing used in pagan times. As has been stated, none of the books of pre-Christian Ireland are now extant, so evidence as to the kind of writing in use must be sought elsewhere. In the absence of books the coinage of a country has often given valuable information in this connection. In the case of Ireland, however, this source of information is lacking; for though metals were worked from very early times and gold was plentiful no trace of a native coinage has been found. Luckily there remain in the stone inscriptions the clearest proofs that the ancient Irish practised a peculiar kind of writing called Ogam.

DESCRIPTION OF OGAM:

Ogam or Ogham was a species of writing the letters of which were a combination of short lines and points on, and at both sides of, a middle or stem line called a *flesc*. In the specimens still remaining this Ogam writing is almost entirely confined to stone inscriptions, the groups of lines and points running along two adjacent sides of a stone with the angular edge for the *flesc*. The arrangement may be understood from a simple diagram.[21]

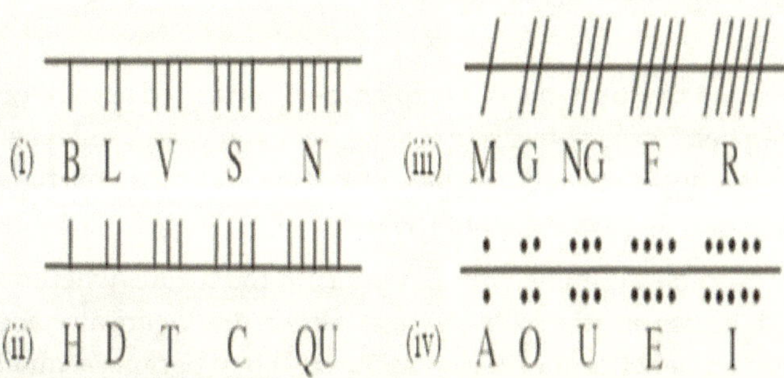

The above diagram shows the Ogam alphabet arranged in four groups. A few other characters are occasionally used. It will be noted that crude as this device for writing is, it is applied with considerable skill and is framed with much ingenuity. The simpler sounds are represented by simpler letters than the more complex. Letters in frequent use like the vowels are the easiest to form. The arrangement of the vowels is different from that used in the Latin and English alphabets but corresponds to the more scientific arrangement adopted by modern phoneticians. It is worth noting that the characters in group (ii) stand for the initial sounds of the Old Irish words for *one, two, three, four, five,* in the order given.

The question of Ogam writing has occupied the attention of many antiquarians and though some of the theories projected by the earlier investigators have been rejected as untenable our knowledge of Ogam at the present time is fairly definite but somewhat limited. It was once thought that Ogam was a cryptic alphabet, but many of the inscriptions have been read by means of the above key which is to be found in the Book of Ballymote. Owing to the fact that a few of the later Ogams have been found with duplicates in Roman letters they have been deciphered independently. As to the distribution of these Ogam inscribed stones it is worthy of note that in Ireland they are found chiefly in the south-west, and in Britain they are confined to those parts where it is known the Irish Gael had settled.[22] Owing to the lack of criteria for dating certain sound-changes in the Irish language it is impossible in the present stage of our knowledge to assign definite chronological limits to these Ogam inscriptions.[23] Mr. Quiggin in his account of Ogam[24]   asserts that the earlier inscriptions cannot be later than the fifth century and if pagan they may be a century or two earlier. All Ogam inscriptions with accompanying Roman letters he would assign to a later period than 500 A.D. with the sole exception of the bilingual inscription of Killen Cormac (Cillin Cormac) which is believed to be earlier than 500 A.D.[25] Over three hundred Ogam inscriptions have been found and where they have not been injured or defaced they can generally be interpreted.

Heroes and druids in the older epics are represented as making constant use of Ogam letters, sometimes inscribing them on wooden staves. The state of civilization depicted in these ancient poems and prose narratives seems to belong mainly to pre-Christian Ireland.

There is some difference in opinion as to the means whereby the Irish discovered the use of letters. One thing is certain, the Ogam alphabet is based on the Latin alphabet. Some think that the Irish first became acquainted with the Roman alphabet through direct trade with the Continent, but it is more probable as MacNeill has shown[26]   that this knowledge was acquired from the Romanized Britons from the first or second century onward. But how or why they invented the Ogam alphabet instead of using the Roman letters, or else Greek ones like the Gauls, is a profound mystery. There can, however, be no doubt that the Ogam alphabet at whatever time invented, is the peculiar possession of the Irish Gael and is to be found only where he had his settlements.

SUMMARY:

From the preceding discussion we may safely conclude:

1. That long before the Christian era the Ancient Irish had developed many useful arts and were skilled and artistic craftsmen.

2. That they had a code of laws that was well suited to the state of society that then existed, and that with slight alterations it was well adapted to meet the requirements of the higher civilization of Christianity. (A corroboration of this view is the well-known fact that at a much later date many of the Anglo-Norman settlers abandoned their own code of laws and adopted the Brehon Code to which they became as much attached as the Irish themselves).

3. That native learning was actively cultivated and systematically developed before the introduction of Christianity.

4. That there was a learned class called druids who were the priests, teachers, poets, historians and judges. (The same man in early times combined in himself all these functions, but in later times there was a tendency to specialize).

5. That the Pagan Irish had a knowledge of letters and that they wrote their learning or part of it in books and cut Ogam inscriptions on stone and wood, but how they obtained this knowledge we have no certain means of determining.

CHAPTER II
THE BEGINNINGS OF CLASSICAL LEARNING

Hitherto our study has been limited to a discussion of native Irish culture influenced but slightly from the outside. Here the attempt is made to trace the beginnings of classical learning. In this connection it is worth noting that Ireland occupies the unique position of being the only part of the Celtic world that was not brought under the sway of Roman arms. The consequence is that she is one of the very few nations of Western Europe whose civilization was free to develop along native lines. Yet it must not be supposed that Ireland remained completely aloof from the Graeco-Roman culture to which the world owes so much.[27] The great difference between Ireland and the other Celtic countries such as Britain and Gaul lies in this: in Gaul the combined forces of Roman arms and Roman culture wiped out almost every trace of native culture, the same is true of the greater part of Britain.[28] In Ireland, on the other hand, Roman learning was introduced in a peaceful manner (at least as early as the fifth century, as will be shown later). Now as we have seen native learning was already developing along national lines, the result was that not only did the native learning continue to flourish unchecked by the arrival of the new learning but the former actually received a fresh impulse,[29] while classical learning was cultivated to an extent that is without parallel in contemporary Europe.[30]

The precise way in which letters reached Ireland and the causes which led to "that remarkable outburst of classical learning towards the close of the sixth century"[31] are matters on which most writers express themselves vaguely, or assume that certain ill-defined influences emanating from Britain or Gaul somehow reached her shores, but at what time or by what means they have not been able to determine.

The introduction of classical learning as well as of Christianity is popularly ascribed to St. Patrick whose missionary work began 432 A.D. This opinion though widespread will not stand a critical examination. It is true, however, that St. Patrick is the first person whose name is associated with the introduction of classical learning of whom it can be said that the writings ascribed to him are really his. In the *Book of Armagh* (completed c. 806 A.D.) there is a document called his "Confession," or apology which was copied by the scribe Torbach from the original.[32] Although the

"Confession" and other writings attributed to St. Patrick may be admitted as genuine, it must not be assumed that the learning for which Ireland became famous during the sixth, seventh and eighth centuries could have been the result of his labours.[33] Most people who have read St. Patrick's writings will admit that he makes no claim to be a scholar but on the contrary he has a very humble opinion of himself and reminds us frequently of his ignorance of letters. As Bury says,[34] "His Latin is as 'rustic' as the Greek of St. Mark and St. Matthew," and Whitley Stokes infers from his writings that he knew no Greek.[35] In this respect St. Patrick was no worse than many of his famous contemporaries and successors, for example—his Latin is no more 'rustic' than that of Gregory of Tours who lived a century later. Indeed St. Patrick's claim to fame rests on higher grounds than those of classical scholarship. He was a preacher and organizer rather than a man of letters. He was a *homo unius libri* but with that book, the Christian Scriptures, he was extraordinarily familiar.[36] Yet some writers have attributed the introduction of learning and even of the Roman alphabet to St. Patrick. It is true that in the *Tripartite Life* there are frequent statements that he wrote *Abgitoria* (usually translated Alphabets) for his noble or bardic converts.[37] It is very probable that these do not mean alphabets, as is usually supposed, like that on the pillar stone of Kilmakedar in Kerry,[38] but *elementa*, the A B C of the Christian Doctrine. This explanation seems justified by the words *Abgitir Crabaid* glossed *initium fidei* in a Würzburg MS.[39] In the Tripartite occur the words, *Aibgitir in Crabaid*—translated the Alphabet of Piety—where a specimen is given of a work so entitled.[40] For these and other reasons which will be stated presently the weight of evidence is against attributing to St. Patrick the introduction of the Roman alphabet or any liberal measure of classical learning.

It has also been suggested[41] that some of the Britons or Gauls who accompanied St. Patrick brought these studies to Ireland, but Meyer thinks this most improbable and dismisses the idea that any missionaries whether Gallic or British introduced classical learning into Ireland. The origin of that deep culture embracing not only the classical authors but also grammar, metrics, and other sciences such as astronomy he would attribute to a much broader and deeper influence.[42]

Basing his argument on a document found among Zimmer's papers, Meyer contends that the seeds of classical learning were sown in Ireland during the first and second decades of the fifth century by Gallic scholars who fled their own country owing to the invasion of the latter by the Goths and other barbarians.[43] The same explanation seems to have occurred to De Jubainville, for he says: "La culture des lettres classiques et latins a cessé en Gaule depuis la conquête germanique au cinquième siècle; *l'Irlande* qu'à cette époque n'a pas encore envahie les barbares des contrées situées à nord-ouest de la Gaule, *paraît avoir donné asile aux hommes d'étude chassés de la Gaule* par les armes et la domination sauvage des Burgundes, des Wisigoths et des Francs."[44] To Meyer, however, we owe the development of this theory. He quotes from a sixth century entry in a Leyden MS. This note states that owing to a barbarian invasion "all the learned men fled from Gaul, and in transmarine parts, *i.e.* in Ireland and wherever they betook themselves, brought about a great advancement of learning to the inhabitants of these regions."[45] This theory is supported by a passage in St. Patrick's "Confession"[46] where evidently replying to the attacks of certain rhetoricians who were hostile to him, the saint exclaims: "You rhetoricians who know not the Lord hear and search who it was that called me up, fool though I be, from the midst of those who call themselves wise and skilled in the law and mighty orators and powerful in everything."[47] Meyer maintains that the reference is to the pagan rhetoricians from Gaul whose arrogant presumption founded on their own learning made them regard with disdain the illiterate apostle of the Scots. His few and forcible epithets well describe the type of rhetorician common in Gaul.

If Meyer's theory is correct, and it seems the most tenable that has been advanced, then we may conclude that Ireland derived her classical learning from Gaul when Gallic scholarship was at its best. This would explain the excellence of the Latin and the acquaintance with Greek which, as we shall show, was exhibited by the Irish scholars who visited the Continent from the time of Columbanus (543–615) to that of Johannes Scottus Eriugena (c. 810–c. 875).

The more one examines this subject the more he is inclined to accept this theory which gets over the difficulty of assuming that the Irish obtained their classical learning from Britain where as Zimmer has shown there was not any classical learning wide and profound enough to produce such results;[48] nor were the High Schools of Gaul a quiet place for learning in the fifth century[49] though Colgan would have us believe—we know not on what authority—that St. Patrick sent St. Olcan to Gaul to study sacred and profane learning so that he might return to Ireland to establish "publicas scholas."[50]

There is nothing improbable in supposing that these rhetoricians should flee to Ireland for safety just as refugee Christians fled to the same island from the persecutions of the Emperor Diocletian more than a century before St. Patrick's time.[51] Indeed Ireland was well known to Roman geographers, though their ideas of its location were rather inaccurate. Tacitus informs us that Ireland is situated between Spain and Britain,[52] a conception which points to direct communication with the Empire. The same author further informs us that the harbours of Ireland were well known to merchants through trade and commerce.[53] As the researches of Mr. George Coffey and Mrs. Greene have shown, intercourse and commerce between Ireland and Gaul had been constant and regular for centuries before the fifth.[54] There were even Gallic mercenaries in the service of Irish kings during the early centuries of our era.[55] Moreover, Irishmen at this time were familiar figures on the Continent. Amongst these may be mentioned Mansuetus, Bishop of Toul about 350 A.D.[56] There can be little doubt that Sedulius, the great Christian poet, author of *Carmen Pascale*, was an Irishman.[57] Sedulius, sometimes called Sedulius the Elder (to distinguish him from another Sedulius who was at Compostella in the eighth century and still another Sedulius who was at Liège in the ninth), flourished between 423–450 A.D.[58] His work treating of the chief events recorded in the Old and New Testament was "the first Christian Epic worthy of the name."[59] Dr. Sigerson by a scholarly analysis[60] of the verse structure traces the influence of the Irish school of prosody referred to in the previous chapter. Though Sedulius wrote in Latin and followed the classical forms of verse, yet he infused into them certain characteristics of Irish poetry, such as systematic alliteration, assonance and rhyme—qualities that reveal the Gael.

Ireland is also credited with the doubtful honour of having given birth to Pelagius and his associate Caelestius.[61] Both flourished in the beginning of the fifth century. Zimmer contended that Pelagius was an Irishman,[62] but Healy shows that he was a British monk of Irish origin.[63] Healy also endeavours to prove that the assumption that Caelestius was an Irishman is based on a misconception.[64] Against this view we must place Meyer's opinion. The latter asserts that whether Pelagius was an Irishman or not "his faithful henchman, Caelestius, he of the plausible tongue, certainly was."[65] The weight of evidence seems to point to the conclusion that one or other, if not both, of these heresiarchs was Irish or at least of Irish descent.

Enough was written to show that some Irish families at least were in reach of a classical literary education and were prompt to grasp it even before the middle of the fifth century.[66] Hence we cannot attribute the introduction of classical learning to St. Patrick as has been so often asserted. Nor can we attribute to St. Patrick the introduction of Christianity itself. According to Zimmer there were missionaries at work in the third century in the southern part of Ireland.[67] It would seem, however, that Zimmer makes too sweeping a statement when he says that Ireland was a Christian land before the fifth century; for, as MacCaffery has pointed out, the Irish Hero Tales which were taken down about the beginning of the eighth century represent the life of the first, second and third centuries and paint the social life as unaffected by Christianity.[68]

That there were some Christians in Ireland before the time of St. Patrick there can be no doubt. Bede distinctly states that Palladius, the predecessor of St. Patrick, was sent by Pope Celestine to the Irish who believed in Christ—"*ad Scottos in Christum credentes.*"[69] Here it should be pointed out that the word *Scoti* or *Scotti* wherever it occurs in writings prior to the tenth century means the *Irish*, and the Irish alone, the inhabitants of Scotia Major (Ireland). Later the term was extended to include the Irish colony in North Britain (Scotia Minor). Eventually the name was still further extended to include the inhabitants of the whole country now called Scotland.[70]

It has been necessary to go into some detail in order to refute a popular fallacy that it was due to the labours of St. Patrick that Ireland owes the introduction of Christianity as well as the beginnings of classical learning. However, as Professor Bury points out, the fact that the foundations of Christianity had been laid sporadically in certain parts of Ireland does not deprive St. Patrick's mission of its eminent significance. He did three things: he organised the Christianity which already existed; he converted many districts which were still pagan, especially in the West; he brought Ireland into connection with the Church of the Empire and made it formally a part of universal Christendom.[71] While as has been shown he did not introduce classical learning, his indirect influence must have been considerable. The very fact that Latin was the ecclesiastical language of the new religion gave it an importance and a dignity. Besides St. Patrick and his fellow workers would naturally help to diffuse a knowledge of ecclesiastical Latin at least in every part of the island which Christianity reached,[72] but it must be remembered that Ireland was not a completely Christian land even at his death.[73] Paganism still lingered in many parts and its influence can be traced in the early native literature,[74] and even in the early Lives of the Irish Saints.[75] To complete the work which he did so much to promote as well as to supply the spiritual wants of the converted, a native ministry was essential. In order to equip such a ministry Christian schools had to be established. Unable to give proper attention to the instruction of these ecclesiastical students, St. Patrick after about twenty years' peripatetic teaching established c. 450 A.D. a school at Armagh of which St. Benin or Benignus was given charge. The primary aim of this school was to train subjects for the priesthood.[76] A knowledge of Latin and perhaps Greek were acquired. To supply the various churches with books there was a special house in which students were employed as scribes.[77]

From what has been said about the presence of Gallic scholars in Ireland we may infer that there were classical schools in existence in certain localities, but in the foundation of the School of Armagh we have the first recorded attempt at the organization of instruction in Christian theology and classical learning in Ireland. We append a list of other schools which the most reliable authorities ascribe to the latter half of the fifth century. It is doubtful whether these were really monastic schools at first for reasons that will be given in the next chapter. It is more likely that they were ecclesiastical seminaries during the time of the First Order of Saints (c. 440–534 A.D.).[78]

The significance of these fifth century schools from the point of view of the present study lies in the fact that they were the precursors of the great monastic schools which sprang up in such numbers in the sixth century. We have good reason for believing that it was in these early schools and by the labours of Gallic scholars and their pupils that the foundations were laid of that classical scholarship that drew the eyes of Europe upon Ireland during the sixth, seventh and eighth and ninth centuries.

IRISH SCHOOLS IN THE FIFTH CENTURY

SCHOOL	DATE	LOCATION	FOUNDER
Ardagh[1a]	—[1b]	Co. Longford	St. Patrick, d. 465 A.D.[1c] and St. Mel, d. 488 A.D.
Ardmore[2a]	—[2b]	Co. Waterford	St. Declan*[2c]
Armagh[3a]	450–5 A.D.[3b]	Co. Armagh	St. Patrick[3c]
Arran[4a]	ante 484 A.D.[4b]	Co. Galway	St. Enda[4c]
Beg Eri[5a]	—[5b]	Co. Wexford	St. Ibar*[5c]
Dysart[6a]	c. 450 A.D.[6b]	Co. Louth	SS. Patrick and Dachonna[6c]
Emly[7a]	—[7b]	Co. Tipperary	St. Ailbe*[7c]
Elphin[8a]	—[8b]	Co. Roscommon	St. Asicus, d. 470 A.D.[8c]
Kildare[9a]	c. 487 A.D.[9b]	Co. Kildare	SS. Brigid, d. 525 A.D.[9c] and Conlaeth, d. 419 A.D.
Louth[10a]	c. 454 A.D.[10b]	Co. Louth	St. Mochta[10c]

Nendrum[11a]	c. 450 A.D.[11b]	Co. Down	St. Caelan or Mochaoi[11c] d. 497–9
Rath Muighe[12a]	—[12b]	Co. Antrim	St. Patrick[12c]
Saul[13a]	—[13b]	Co. Down	St. Patrick[13c]
Slane[14a]	—[14b]	Co. Meath	St. Patrick[14c]
Seir[15a]	—[15b]	King's Co.	St. Ciaran,* the Elder[15c]
Trim[16a]	—[16b]	Co. Meath	St. Patrick[16c]

For a discussion of the chronology of SS. Declan, Ibar, Ailbe and Ciaran the Elder, see Power, Rev. Patrick, *Lives of SS. Declan and Mocuda*, pp. xix–xxii, *Irish Texts Series*.

1a. Conyngham, D. P., *Irish Saints and Martyrs*, p. 540. Conyngham relies mainly on Walter Harris's ed. of Ware's *Monasticon Hiberniae* and Lanigan's *Ecclesiastical History of Ireland*. 1b. Unknown. 1c. St. Patrick's death, see Conyngham, D. P., *op. cit.* p. 2; St. Mell's *op. cit.* p. 117.

For the various dates assigned to St. Patrick's death, see Healy, John. *Life and Writings of St Patrick*, pp. 635–7. Bury, J. B. *op. cit.* p. 206 places his death as early as 461 A.D., while the *Annals of the Four Masters*, I., pp. 154–6 give the traditional date as 493 A.D. Modern scholars are inclined to accept one of the earlier dates as the more probable.

2a. Conyngham, D. P., *op. cit.* p. 541. 2b. Unknown. 2c. Power P., *op. cit.* pp. xix–xxii.

3a and 3b. Healy, John, *Ireland's Saints and Scholars*, p. 114 gives 455 A.D. as the date of foundation, the Four Masters give 457 A.D. I, p. 142. Bury, J. B., places the date of foundation as early as 444 A.D. *op. cit.* p. 154. 3c. See Note 1c above.

4a , 4b , and 4c . Conyngham, D. P., *op. cit.* p. 182. See also Healy, John, for an account of the School of St. Enda. *op. cit.*

5a and 5b . Conyngham, D. P., *op. cit.* p. 538. 5c . See Note 1c above.

6a , 6b and 6c . For this and other monasteries see Article by (Rev.) Laurence P. Murray, *Monasteries of County Louth*, in the *Louth Journal of Archaeology*, I, pp. 22–36.

7a . See Healy's account of this school, *op. cit.* 7b . Unknown.

7c . The *Annals of Ulster,* sub anno 526 record St. Ailbe's death, but see Note 2c above.

8a , 8b , and 8c . Healy, John, *op. cit.* 161.

9a , 9b , and 9c . Healy, John, *op. cit.* p. 132, gives 527 A.D. as the date of foundation. The *Chronicon Scottorum* gives 510 A.D.; but this is evidently too late, as St. Brigid died in 525 A.D., according to the Chronology in Miss Hull's *Early Christian Ireland,* introductory pages. St. Conlaeth died in 519 A.D. Conyngham, D. P., *op. cit.* p. 133. The same author places the date of her birth at 453 A.D., so it is fair to assume that the date of the foundation of this school is 487 A.D. and not 467 A.D.

10a , 10b , 10c . Murray, L. P., *ibid.*

11 a and 11 b. Reeves, Wm., *Ecclesiastical Antiquities of Down, Connor, and Dromore,* p. 10; 11 c. Reeves, Wm., *op. cit.* p. 138.

12 a, 12 b, and 12 c. Founded by St. Patrick according to the tradition accepted by Conyngham, *op. cit.* p. 540, and others, but more probably at a later date by St. Comgall, d. 601 A.D. See Reeves' *Ecc. Antiq.,* p. 70.

13a , 13 b, and 13 c. Conyngham, D. P., *op. cit.* p. 540.

14a , 14b , and 14c . Conyngham, D. P., *op. cit.* p. 539.

15a , 15b , and 15c . Conyngham, D. P., *op. cit.* p. 538.

16a , 16b , and 16c . Conyngham, D. P., *op. cit.* p. 539.

This list does not claim to be complete. The above dates agree with those given by the most careful authorities. The four saints whose names are marked (*) are usually called the pre-Patrician Saints. Their chronology is very difficult. Some authorities place them as early as the fourth century and some as late as the sixth.

CHAPTER III
IRISH MONASTICISM

As the organization of the Irish monastic schools was so intimately connected with the Irish monastic system it is impossible to form a clear idea of the character, aims, curriculum, or the scope of scholarship of these schools without some reference to Irish monasticism and its relation to other types of monasticism.

Monasticism in general is a system of living that owes its origin to those tendencies of human nature which are summed up in the words mysticism and asceticism. Mysticism may be defined as the efforts to give effect to the craving for union with the Deity even in this life; and asceticism, as the effort to give effect to the hankering after an ever progressive purification of the soul, and an atoning for sin by the renunciation and self-denial of things lawful.[79] These two tendencies would appear to be inseparable from humanity, because though not always called into activity, they are always liable to be invoked, and in all ages and among all peoples they have frequently asserted themselves.[80] In one form or another monasticism had appealed to people of various countries long before it became associated with Christianity. In the early years of Christianity monasticism took a definite shape in Syria, Egypt and Armenia. From Egypt and Syria it was brought to Rome about the middle of the fourth century by Athanasius, the great champion of the Divinity of Christ; by Honorius, the founder of the island monastery of Lerins; and by Cassian whose "Institutes" were a kind of manual for all the earlier monasteries of the West.[81]

As to the origin of Irish Monasticism opinions are divided: some have ascribed it to an Eastern origin, while others insist that it can be directly traced to Gaul. The most commonly accepted view is that of Mr. Willis Bund[82] which ascribes to it a purely indigenous development. As such general statements are at best but partly true and utterly fail to give an adequate idea of the characteristics of Irish monasticism we propose to examine the subject in the light derived from such native sources of information as:

1. The Irish Monastic Rules,[83]

2. The Lives of the Early Irish Saints,[84]

3. Ecclesiastical History, and

4. Social and Political History.

From the first and second sources we shall learn much about the spirit of monastic life, its ideals, obligations, and daily routine. From the third and fourth sources, and incidentally from the other two, we learn much about the relation which existed between the monastery and the community in which it was located.

An examination of Irish Monastic Rules, so far as they have come down to us, reveals the fact that they are not identical with any Eastern or Western Code. In the general severity of their regulations they are found, on comparison, to resemble the former rather than the latter. It was doubtless this austerity that caused the Irish Rules to give way eventually before the milder Rule of St. Benedict.[85] It is possible, however, that the ideas and literature of Gallic and Egyptian monasticism may have influenced to some extent the development of Irish monasticism.[86]

Whether Irish monasticism was of native origin or not there can be little doubt that British monasticism exercised a very potent and direct influence on its development. In an Irish document which is generally accepted as historical, we are informed that there were Three Orders of Saints.[87] The First Order flourished c. 440–534 A.D. Many of the saints in this Order lived in the time of St. Patrick. They were all bishops and founders of churches. Their number was 350 and included Britons, Romans, Franks and Scots. The Second Order (534–572 A.D.) was made up of few bishops and many priests: they numbered 300. Unlike the First Order these refused the services of women separating them from their monasteries. They received a Mass from SS. David, Gillas, and Docus the Britons. The Third Order consisted of holy priests and a few bishops. The number of this Order was 100; they dwelt in desert places living mainly on herbs and water; they depended upon alms and possessed no private property.

The Second Order interests us especially as in all probability the monasteries owe their origin to its members. Whether St. Patrick actually founded monasteries is uncertain. We know that he spent some years at Lerins, the island monastery of the Mediterranean, but his life was too full of missionary labours to have time for the foundation and government of monasteries.[88] In strong contrast with the First Order who were mainly foreigners, the Second Order of Saints were all natives of Ireland. However, they came under the influence of British monasticism in two ways. We have seen above that three British or Welsh saints visited Ireland during this period, and indeed so did several others.[89] Of equal importance is the fact that several Irish saints visited Britain about this time. In South Wales there were two centres of attraction, Llancarvon under St. Cadoc and Menevia under St. David.[90] St. Finnian of Clonard, "the tutor of the Saints of Erin," was a pupil of St. Cadoc at Llancarvon, as was St. Cainnech. Maedoc was a pupil of St. David's, as were Modomnoc and Scuithin, while we hear of Finnian of Clonard, Declan, Bairre and Senan as visitors there.[91] The saints of the North of Ireland tended to gravitate towards a monastery in the territory of the Niduari Picts, sometimes called Strathclyde, in the South-west of Scotland. This monastery was called Whitern (Rosnat in Irish sources). Among the Irish saints who visited Whitern are SS. Enda, Tighernach, Eoghan of Ardstraw and Finnian of Movilla.[92]

INFLUENCE OF CLONARD MONASTERY:

About the middle of the sixth century a great monastic movement took rise from the monastery established at Clonard by Finnian c. 525 A.D.[93] Under him were trained for missionary work many of the most illustrious fathers of the Irish church including the "Twelve Apostles of Erin,"[94] viz. Ciaran of Seir, Ciaran of Clonmacnoise, Columba (Colum Cille), Brendan of Clonfert, Brendan of Birr, Columba or Colman of Terryglass, Molaise of Devenish, Canice of Aghaboe, Ruadan of Lorrha, Mobi of Glasnevin, Sinnel of Cleenish, and Ninnidh or Nennius of Inishmacsaint.[95] According to another authority, the names of Finnian of Clonard, Finnian of Movilla, and Comgall of Bangor are substituted for those of Ciaran of Seir, Molaise of Devenish, and Sinnel of Cleenish.[96] The remaining nine names occur in both lists. These men going forth in all directions founded numerous monasteries and schools which afterwards became famous throughout Europe.[97] St. Columba (Colum Cille) styled in an old record *"Monasteriorum Pater et Fundator"* is said to have founded 300 monasteries. Even allowing for the poetic imagination of the early chronicler, it is significant that Reeves in his investigations was able to compile a list of at least 90 monasteries founded by, or dedicated to, this saint. Of this number 37 were located in Ireland, 32 amongst the Scots (of Alba) and 21 amongst the Picts, *i.e.* 53 in the country now called Scotland.[98] It was mainly through the efforts of these saints that Ireland was completely converted to the Christian faith.[99] It would appear that after St. Patrick's death the druids recovered some of their former influence and exerted themselves to the utmost to retard and limit the spread of the new faith.[100] Thanks to the zeal and energy of the saints of this Second Order the influence of the druids was completely broken down, though the druids still lingered on obscurely and feebly many generations.[101]

When monasticism became general in the sixth century most, if not all, of those ecclesiastical seminaries which we have listed as being founded in the fifth century, became monastic schools. Some of them such as the School of Armagh attained a high degree of excellence ranking with Clonard, Bangor, and the other great schools which date from the sixth century. We give a list of the better-known monastic schools which were founded during the sixth and seventh centuries, the most famous being printed in CAPITALS. These schools were all established in Ireland by Irishmen, who, as far as we have been able to discover, received their own education for the most part in schools already in existence in Ireland. This list makes no pretence to completeness. According to the calculations of Sir James Ware the number of famous schools in Ireland amounted to 164.[102] Another writer[103] gives the names of 168 monasteries founded prior to 900 A.D. Even this list is incomplete. We have checked this latter list for Co. Louth with one compiled by a recent reliable investigator[104] with the result that 19 or 20 should be credited to Co. Louth whereas there are only 2 out of the 168 so accredited. Similarly, we find only 4 monasteries ascribed to St. Columba while, as we have shown, Reeves found 37 monasteries in Ireland whose foundation is accredited to this energetic saint. As we have reason to believe that all these monasteries had schools, we can easily see how abundant were the facilities for acquiring such an education as these schools provided.

MONASTIC SCHOOLS FOUNDED IN IRELAND
BETWEEN 500 AND 700 A.D.

SCHOOL	DATE	LOCATION	FOUNDER
Aghaboe[1a]	—[1b]	Co. Kilkenny	St. Canice, 528–600 A.D.[1c]
BANGOR[2a]	559 A.D.[2b]	Co. Down	St. Comgall d. 601–2 A.D.[2c]
Birr[3a]	c. 560 A.D.[3b]	King's Co.	St. Brendan of Birr[3c] ? 490–573 A.D.
Cleenich[4a]	6th cent.[4b]	Co. Fermanagh	St. Sinnel[4c]
Clogher[5a]	—[5b]	Co. Tyrone	St. Macartin, c. 506 A.D.[5c]
CLONARD[6a]	c. 520 A.D.[6b]	Co. Meath	St. Finnian, 470–549 A.D.[6c]
Clonenagh[7a]	c. 548 A.D.[7b]	Queen's Co.	St. Fintan, 525–592 A.D.[7c]

Clonfert[8a]	553–7 A.D.[8b]	Co. Galway	St. Brendan the Navigator[8c] 484–577 A.D.
Cork[9a]	—[9b]	Co. Cork	St. Finnbar, 5 7 0 – 6 3 0 A.D.[9c]
CLONMACNOISE[10a]	544–8 A.D.[10b]	King's Co.	St. Ciaran, d. 549 A.D.[10c]
Cluainfois[11a]	c. 500 A.D.[11b]	Co. Galway	St. Iarlaith, c ? 510 A.D.[11c]
Devenish[12a]	530 A.D.[12b]	Co. Fermanagh	St. Molaise, d. 563–71 A.D.[12c]
Derry[13a]	545–6 A.D.[13b]	Co. Derry	St. Columba, 5 2 0 – 5 9 7 A.D.[13c]
Dromore[14a]	c. 500 A.D.[14b]	Co. Down	St. Colman[14c]
Durrow[15a]	553 A.D.[15b]	King's Co.	St. Columba, 5 2 0 – 5 9 7 A.D.[15c]
Glasnevin[16a]	—[16b]	Co. Dublin	St. Mobi, d. 544 A.D.[16c]
Glendalough[17a]	—[17b]	Co. Wicklow	St. Kevin, d 618–22 A.D.[17c]
Inishmacsaint[18a]	—[18b]	Co. Fermanagh	St. Ninnidh, d. post 530 A.D.[18c]
Kells[19a]	550 A.D.[19b]	Co. Meath	St. Columba, 5 2 0 – 5 9 7 A.D.[19c]
Kilkenny[20a]	—[20b]	Co. Kilkenny	St. Canice, 528–600 A.D.[20c]
LISMORE[21a]	635 A.D.[21b]	Co. Waterford	S t . Carthach[21c]
MONASTERBOICE[22a]	c. 500 A.D.[22b]	Co. Louth	St. Buite, c. 521 A.D.[22c]

Mayo[23a]	655 A.D.[23b]	Co. Mayo	St. Colman[23c]
Movilla[24a]	540–55 A.D.[24b]	Co. Down	St. Finnian[24c]
MUNGRET[25a]	c. 551 A.D.[25b]	Co. Limerick	St. Nessan, d. 551 A.D.[25c]
Ros-Ailithir[26a]	6th cent.[26b]	Co. Cork	St. Fachtna[26c]
Swords[27a]	—[27b]	Co. Dublin	St. Columba, 520–597 A.D.[27c]
Scattery Is.[28a]	c. 537 A.D.[28b]	Co. Clare	St. Senan[28c]
Terryglass[29a]	634 A.D.[29b]	Co. Tipperary	St. Colman of Terriglass[29c]
Tuam[30a]	—[30b]	Co. Galway	St. Iarlaith, c. 545 A.D.[30c]

1a . Warren, F. E., *op. cit.* pp. 14, 15. 1b . Unknown. 1c . Conyngham, D. P., *op. cit.* p. 268. *ibid.* Joyce, P. W. *Short History of Ireland*, p. 180, gives (517–600).

2a . Plummer, Charles, *op. cit.* I, p. lxxix. 2b . Joyce, P. W., *Concise History of Ireland*, p. 82. 2c . *Revue Celtique*, XXX, p. 113.

3a , 3b , 3c . Plummer, C., *op. cit.* I, xlii.

4a , 4b , 4c . Conyngham, D. P., *op. cit.* p. 541.

5a , 5b . Conyngham, D. P., *op. cit.* p. 541. 5c . *op. cit.* p. 132.

6a , 6b , 6c . Joyce, P. W., *Con. Hist. of Ir.*, p. 92.

7a , 7b , 7c . Healy, John, *Ireland's Ancient Schools and Scholars*, p. 404, but Plummer, C., *op. cit.* I, lxx, gives 603 A.D. as the date of St. Fintan's death.

8a , 8b , 8c . Plummer, C., *op. cit.* p. I, xxiv.

9a , 9b , 9c . Joyce, P. W., *Con. Hist, of Ir.*, p. 92; Conyngham, D. P., *op. cit.* p. 329.

10a . Plummer, C., *op. cit.* I, p. lxiv. 10b . Chronicles give no date, *ibid.* 10c . Dalton, Canon, *Hist. of Ireland*, I, 71.

11a , 11b , 11c . Healy, John, *op. cit.* p. 160.

12a , 12b , 12c . Plummer, C., *op. cit.* I, p. lxxiv.

13a , 13b , 13c . Hull, Eleanor, *Early Christian Ireland*, Chronological Table; Dalton, Canon, *op. cit.* I, p. 62.

14a , 14b , 14c . Reeves, Wm., *Ecclesiastical Antiquities*, p. 138.

15a , 15b , 15c . Reeves, Wm., *Adamnan's Vita Columbae*, p. 276; Warren, F. E., *op. cit.* pp. 14, 15.

16a , 16b , 16c . Warren, F. E., *op. cit.* pp. 14, 15.

17a , 17b , 17c . Plummer, C., *op. cit.* I, p. xxxiii; Joyce, P. W., *Concise History of Ireland*, p. 92.

18a , 18b , 18c . Warren, F. E., *op. cit.* pp. 14, 15; Conyngham, D. P., *op. cit.* p. 541.

19a , 19b , 19c . Reeves, Wm., *Adamnan*, p. 276.

20a , 20b , 20c . Plummer, C., *op. cit.* I, p. lxxix; Joyce, P. W., *op. cit.* p. 92.

21a , 21b , 21c . Joyce, P. W., *op. cit.* p. 81; Dalton, *op. cit.* I, p. 74.

22a , 22b , 22c . Macalister, R. A. S., *Muiredach, Abbot of Monasterboice.* Introduction, Murray, L. P., *op. cit.*

23a , 23b , 23c . *Chronicon Scottorum*, p. 104; Conyngham, D. P., *op. cit.* p. 543.

24a , 24b , 24c . Reeves, Wm., *Ecclesiastical Antiquities*, p. 138.

25a , 25b , 25c . Joyce, P. W., *Concise Hist. of Ireland*, p. 92.

26a , 26b , 26c . Joyce, P. W., *ibid.*; Conyngham, D. P., *op. cit.* p. 541.

27a , 27b , 27c . Reeves, Wm., *Adamnan*, p. 279.

28a , 28b , 28c . Joyce, P. W., *op. cit.* p. 81.

29a , 29b , 29c . Warren, F. E., *op. cit.* pp. 14, 15; Conyngham, D. P., *op. cit.* p. 542.

30a , 30c . Healy, John, *op. cit.* p. 160. 30b . Date of the foundation is uncertain. Conyngham, D. P., *op. cit.* p. 543 states that it was founded in the Fifth Century.

EDUCATIONAL SIGNIFICANCE OF THE ORGANIZATION OF THE IRISH CHURCH.

From what has been said about the spread of monasticism in Ireland in the sixth century it is evident that the whole organization of the Church in Ireland was being placed on a monastic basis. The importance of this type of organization from an educational standpoint will be evident when we recall the actual condition of society at this particular period. Closely related to the monastic character of the Irish Church was its missionary character.

How far reaching the influence of the Irish Monastic Church was, can be judged from a brief survey of the distribution of Irish monasteries in Britain and on the Continent. A list of 122 monasteries founded by Irish monks in Scotland, in England and on the Continent was collected by Colgan in a lost work of which the index has been preserved and printed.[105] Another writer has shown that Ireland sent 115 missionaries into Germany, 45 into France, 44 into England, 36 into Belgium, 25 into Scotland and 13 into Italy. [106] According to the testimony of Jonas, biographer of Columbanus, about 620 missionaries went into Bavaria from Luxeuil, the headquarters of the missionary work of Columbanus. No doubt, some of these were natives of Gaul, but there must have been many Irish amongst them. Miss Stokes gives the names of 63 missionaries who in the seventh century spread the Columban Rule from Luxeuil.[107] In the light of these facts we see how just is the judgment of Green, the English historian, when he declared that as the Irish Church overflowed its own territorial limits and invaded the Continent of Europe, it was for a time doubtful whether the monastic ideal of Christendom would come from a Celtic or from an Italian source, whether it would be represented by the Rules of SS. Columba and Columbanus, or that of St. Benedict.[108]

IMPOSSIBILITY OF COMPILING A COMPLETE LIST OF MONASTIC SCHOOLS AND SCHOLARS:

The number of monastic schools and scholars given in the preceding section though at first sight somewhat startling is really an under-estimate. This assertion is based on the following considerations:—

1. The desire which prevailed in the early centuries of Christianity to imitate even the accidental features of the Apostolic system naturally suggested the adoption of the number *twelve* in the adjustment of missionary societies. Thus we find it recorded that in Clonard the "Twelve Apostles of Erin" were educated. St. Columba set out about 562 A.D. with *twelve* companions to convert the Picts. St. Columbanus with *twelve* brethren left Ireland about 612 to undertake his great missionary work on the Continent. St. Killian was the chief of a company of *twelve* who founded a monastic institution in Würzburg. St. Eloquius, disciple of St. Fursa, with *twelve* companions whose names are preserved, propagated the Gospel in Belgium.[109] Thus except in the case of the founders of monasteries there is a very natural tendency to overlook the other workers, sometimes their names are not even recorded.

2. During the Danish incursions of the ninth and tenth centuries many of the Irish monasteries were destroyed and the monks went to Europe and set

up monasteries wherever they settled. Sometimes they carried their books with them, but more frequently their libraries were burned or "drowned" by the pagan invaders who hated Christianity and learning, thus the Irish Annals and other documents are very defective as a means of supplying the necessary data for the compilation of a tolerably complete list.[110]

3. Even when the names of Irish missionaries are recorded in Continental MSS. there is often a difficulty in recognising an Irish name in its Continental dress. Many of the Irish monks who went abroad were "re-christened," sometimes Biblical names like Joseph or Isaias were adopted, or the Irish name was latinized to make it more euphonious to Continental ears. Hence we find *Moengal* figuring as Marcellus, just as *Maelmuire* appears as Marianus and Mylerius, *Maelmeadhog* as Malachy, *Giolla Iosa* and even *Cellach* become Gelasius, *Giolla an Coimded* figures as Germanus, *Tuathal* as Tutilo, *Domnall* or *Donal* as Donatus, *Aed* as Aidan and Hugh, *Siadhal* as Sedulius, *Cellach* sometimes became Gall, while others chose to remain anonymous or describe themselves vaguely as *Exul*, or *Hibernicus*, or *Scottus*. In the Continental libraries there are many MSS. in Irish script and the scribes have concealed their identity in the vague manner just described.[111]

4. Naturally there were many others whose work was teaching rather than writing, consequently there is no record in such cases. Columba and Columbanus were lucky in having biographers but many others were less fortunate.

GEOGRAPHICAL DISTRIBUTION OF IRISH MONASTIC SCHOOLS:

We give a partial list of the better-known monastic institutions which were at one and the same time advance posts of civilization and centres of Christian learning. Many of these date from that great period of Irish missionary activity, the seventh century.

SCOTLAND:

Almost the whole of the country now called Scotland was converted to Christianity by Irish missionaries. With the foundation of the monastery of Iona in 563 A.D. by St. Columba, *"pater et fundator monasteriorum,"* began a period of great monastic activity in Britain. Reeves found that 63 monasteries were founded by or dedicated to St. Columba; of these 32 were in the territory occupied by the Scots and 21 were among the Picts. [112] Other important monasteries were Deer founded by St. Drostan, a disciple of St. Columba, Lismore founded by St. Moluag in 592 A.D., and Righ-Monadh or Kilrimont founded by St. Canice near the place where St. Andrew's University is now located.[113] There were also numerous small monasteries on the islands round the Scottish coast.[114] The beneficent influence exercised by these foundations as civilizing and educational agencies is acknowledged by modern Scottish historians.[115]

ENGLAND:

Just as Iona was the great headquarters of monastic activity for Scotland, so Lindisfarne founded by the Irish St. Aidan in 635 A.D. became the base of operations for the Irish missionaries in the North of England, especially in Northumbria. At this time Northumbria was an extensive kingdom extending as far south as the Humber and into modern Scotland as far north as the Firth of Forth. To the influence of Aidan and other Irish monks we trace the foundation of Lindisfarne, Coldingham, Mailros, Lastingham, in Northumbria, Ripon and Streanshalch (now Whitby) in Yorkshire, Burgh Castle in Suffolk, St. Bees in Lancashire, Malmesbury among the West Saxons, Bosham or Bosanham in Sussex, and "Glastonbury of the Gael" in Somerset.[116] In most histories the missionary work of St. Augustine is grossly exaggerated and the important missionary and educational work of the Irish monks is either completely ignored or accorded an amount of space utterly out of proportion to its importance.[117]

IRISH FOUNDATIONS ON THE CONTINENT:

In *Netherlands*: Namur, Liège, Gueldres, Fosse, Haumont, Soignes.[118]

In *France*: Remiremont, Lure, Besançon, Poitiers (f. 511), Bezieres, Romain-Moutier, Brezille, Cusance, St. Ursanne, Fleury (f. 629), St. Riquier (f. 625), Jouarre, Reuil, Rébais (f. 634), Faremoutier, St. Maur-des-Fossés, Lagny, Montier-la-Celle, Caudabec, Hautvilliers, Montier-en-Der, St. Salaberga, Meaux, St. Saens, Fontennelle, Jumieges, Stavelot (f. 656), Corbie (f. 662), Anegray, Luxeuil (f. 599), Fontaines, Ferrières (f. 630), Peronne (f. 650) or *Perrona Scottorum*, Toul, Amboise, Beaulieu, Strasbourg, in addition to the countless and nameless *Hospitalia Scottorum* alluded to in the Capitularies of Charles the Bald in 846 A.D.[119]

In *Germany and Switzerland*: Hohenaug, Würzburg, Memmingen, Erfurt, Freyburg, Schuttern, Ettenheimünster, Mentz, Cologne, Nuremburg, Altomünster, Ratisbon or Regensburg, Constance, St. Gall (f. 614), Mont St. Victor, Bregens (f. 610), Reichenau, Seckingen.[120]

In *Italy*: Bobbio (f. 612), Taranto, Lucca, Faenza, Fiesole.[121]

RELATION OF THE IRISH MONASTIC CHURCH TO THE ROMAN CHURCH:

The preceding section will enable us to understand what an important influence from a religious, as well as from an educational, standpoint the Irish monastic system began to exercise throughout the West of Europe. The relation which existed between the Irish Church and the Roman Church has given rise to considerable polemic discussion. Indeed there are so many points in common between the Irish monastic church of the sixth, seventh, and eighth centuries and the British or Welsh church of the same period that both are often spoken of as the "Celtic Church" in contradistinction to the Roman Church. This distinction is based not on any essential difference of doctrine[122] but on certain differences of ritual, liturgy, and discipline. As we have shown the Irish monastic system extended far beyond the territorial limits occupied by the Celtic race. Hence when we refer to the Celtic Church we have in mind a widespread organization rather than a locality, and we emphasize differences of custom and not essentials of dogma. The differences that existed between the Roman Church and the Celtic Church with regard to the date of Easter and to the tonsure of the monks gave rise to an important controversy in the seventh century.[123]

THE CALCULATION OF EASTER:

Prior to the Council of Nice 325 A.D. the date of Easter in the nascent Celtic Church harmonized with that of the Roman Church. Owing, however, to isolation the Celtic Church had never adopted the various alterations and improvements which on astronomical—not on theological—grounds had been accepted by the Continental Church.[124]

THE TONSURE CONTROVERSY:

The Roman tonsure was formed by shaving the top of the head in a circle leaving a crown of hair around it. The Eastern tonsure, sometimes called the Pauline tonsure, was total. The Celtic tonsure was formed by shaving all the hair in front of a line drawn from ear to ear.[125] In the controversy of the seventh century the Roman party traced their form to St. Peter and attributed that of their opponents to Simon Magus.[126] The Irish form, *ab aure ad aurem*, existed in St. Patrick's time[127] and was probably druidical in origin.[128]

These two questions, though in themselves of minor importance, gave rise to a controversy of many years' duration. Eventually the Roman practice was adopted by the whole Celtic Church, but not without a struggle, some localities clinging tenaciously to the traditional usage long after the general acceptance of the Continental practice. The Southern Irish were the first to conform. Having received an admonition from Pope Honorius they convened a Synod about 630 A.D. and as a result of their deliberations decided to adopt the Roman usage. The North of Ireland held out much longer, being influenced by Iona and its dependent monasteries in Ireland. [129] The dates at which the different parts of the Celtic Church conformed with the Roman practice in regard to the celebration of Easter are given below.[130] Possibly the coronal form of tonsure was adopted at the same time.

YEAR.—DISTRICT AFFECTED BY THE CHANGE:

630 A.D.	South of Ireland.
664	Northumbria converted by Irish missionaries from Iona.
692	North of Ireland.
705	East Devon and Somerset, the Celts under Wessex.
710	The Picts of Scotland.
716–718	Iona.
721	Strathclyde, the South-west of Scotland.
768	North Wales.
777	South Wales.
909	Parts of Cornwall.

EFFECT OF THE EASTER CONTROVERSY ON EDUCATION:

The Irish monks who visited the Continent, as well as the adherents of the Roman usage in Britain, advocated and even urged the necessity of conforming to the Continental practices, but their compatriots did not yield without a struggle. As we have shown, certain parts of Britain in which the Celtic Church held sway were even more reluctant to give up the traditional usages. So far as the general interests of education are concerned this controversy had a somewhat harmful effect. It diverted the attention of scholars from matters of greater moment and created a certain prejudice against those Irish teachers who were not prepared to give up the cherished customs of the founders of their monasteries. For example, after the Synod of Whitby in 664 A.D. when Celtic usage was abolished, St. Colman and a number of Anglo-Saxon followers retired from Lindisfarne and founded a monastery on Inisbofinn, an island off the west coast of Ireland. It must not, however, be assumed that the Irish influence in England ceased with the departure of St. Colman and his followers. At the Synod of Whitby some of the most vigorous advocates of the Roman usage were Irishmen, while amongst the Anglo-Saxons there were many champions of the Celtic usage.[131] For at least thirty years after the Synod of Whitby the Irish influence was felt. A native ministry having been trained the Irish monks had accomplished their work.[132] In one respect the Easter controversy had a good effect on learning. It led to a careful study of the computation and astronomy and created the necessity of becoming familiar with all the classical and ecclesiastical literature which was calculated to throw any light on that vexed question. The consequence of this study was that the Irish monks became the greatest astronomers of the seventh, eighth and ninth centuries. It is enough to read the Paschal Epistle of Cummian Fada (d. 661) [133] or the famous letter of Dungal who in 810 A.D. was asked by Charles the Great to explain the double eclipse of the sun which was supposed to have occurred in that year,[134] to be convinced of the superiority of their scholarship.

ORGANIZATION OF THE IRISH MONASTERY ON A TRIBAL BASIS:

In marked contrast with the other Western churches which were organized on a national and episcopal basis the Irish Church was tribal and monastic. This was quite natural. The conversion of the chieftain was followed by the conversion of the clansmen and a tribal character was thus given to the nascent church.[135] At an early date the Irish Church took a monastic form which accorded so well with the native social system. The abbot became chief of an ecclesiastical clan most of whose members were descended from the same common ancestor as the abbot himself. No wonder the native name for the monastic community was *muintir*, usually translated *familia*.[136] Even the successor of the abbot—the *coarb*, literally heir—could often claim lineal descent from the same chieftain as the abbot whom he succeeded. Of course, as the abbot was unmarried, there could be no direct lineal succession from the first abbot, but there was a succession in the manner indicated. There was thus a close resemblance between the succession of the abbot and that of the chieftain. The successor of the chieftain was not necessarily his son, but a member of the clan by whom he was selected on account of his personal fitness for the position. In the case of the monastery of Iona it has been noted that Columba and thirteen of his successors were descended from a common ancestor, an Irish chief named Conall Gulban.[137] The monastic family consisted of *fratres*: those of tried devotion were called *seniores*; those who were strong for labour were *operarii fratres*; and those under instruction were *juniores, alumni,* or *pueri familiares.* Besides the congregation—*collectio*—of professed members there were usually present *peregrini,* sometimes called *proselyti, poenitentes,* or *hospites* whose sojourn was of varied duration.[138]

The number of officers was relatively small, the more important being the *abbot,* the *prior,* the *episcopus,* the *scriba,* and the *Erinach* or *Airchinneach.* The *abbot* was the superior of the monastic family and frequently had several houses under his supreme control. He generally lived at the mother house. The branch houses were governed by local superiors called *priors* who were subject to removal by the abbot. There was also a prior at the mother house who assisted the abbot and took his place in administration when his superior was absent. The prior in this latter capacity is sometimes styled *custos monasterii,* sometimes *oeconomus,* and in the Irish Annals, *Fertighis.*[139]

An interesting fact in connection with the Irish monastic organization is that the abbot was not necessarily a bishop.[140] In matters of discipline and jurisdiction the abbot was supreme whether he was a bishop or not. But if he were not a bishop there were certain duties which he could not perform. The bishop (episcopus) as such and in virtue of his office performed such functions as administration of Confirmation and Holy Orders just as at present. Of course the abbot was frequently a bishop and consequently was vested with correspondingly increased powers.[141]

The abbot sometimes combined the office of scribe with his other duties. The special work of the scribe will be dealt with later; here it is sufficient to note that the office of scribe was held in such honour that we often find it recorded of a certain saint that he was an excellent scribe, while as if of secondary importance, it is added that he was an abbot, or bishop.[142]

The lands belonging to the monastery or church were usually managed by an officer called an erinach, or herenach (in Irish, Airchinneach). The erinach, who was usually a layman, first deducted his own stipend and gave the residue for the purposes intended—the support of the church, or the relief of the poor. It was generally understood to be the duty of the erinach to keep the church clean and in proper repair, and the grounds in order. There were erinachs in connection with nearly all the monasteries and churches.[143] Lay erinachs were usually tonsured.[144]

REVENUES AND MEANS OF SUPPORT.

The monasteries derived their means of support from a variety of sources, the chief being: *Lands, Tithes, Fees* and *Dues,* and *Gifts.*

By far the most important of all these means of support were the lands attached to the monastery. These lands, called *Termon* lands in Ireland, derived their name in all probability from the *termini*, pillar stones, or crosses set up to mark their boundaries within which there was right of sanctuary, and a freedom from the taxes and tributes of the secular chieftains.[145] These lands were tilled by the monks themselves and formed the staple support of the establishment.[146] It was a maxim in all the primitive monasteries that the monks support themselves by the labour of their own hands. The mendicant orders, who depended largely upon alms were a later institution, first introduced into Ireland about 1225 A.D.[147] The monastic lands were sometimes increased by special grants from kings, or chiefs. These special grants when added to the foundation grant sometimes made up an extensive territory.[148] When the lands became too large for the community to work, a portion of them was rented to tenants. Part of the duty of the erinach was to collect the rents and other tributes from the tenants.[149] Ordinarily the monastery was a self-supporting institution. The community produced everything they needed for food, clothing, and shelter. They owed little to society in general but society owed much to them.[150] There was no privileged class in these early monasteries. All who were physically fit had to take part in the manual labour, nor were the scribes or even the abbot exempt.[151]

In parts of the *Senchus Mór*,[152] one of the ancient books of law, it is prescribed as a duty of society to pay tithes, as well as to bestow alms and first fruits to the Church, but tithes were not generally nor regularly paid until after the Norman invasion in 1172 A.D.[153] Another subsidiary, but occasionally substantial, means of support was the dues paid by the tribe to the abbot for the performance of various religious functions.[154] The Brehon Laws lay down specifically the reciprocal obligations of the clergy and laity in this manner.[155] In this connection[156] it should be pointed out that owing to its position in the native social system "the Church in Ireland never became as in other lands by turns the servant, the ally, or the master of the State. It was the companion of the people, and an important element in the national life."

Gifts, or voluntary offerings, were a further source of income, but a fluctuating one, depending largely on the location of the monastery, its reputation, the social condition of its patrons, and a variety of other accidental circumstances. Almost all persons who visited a monastery left something of value, if their means permitted. In early times the offerings, like other payments, were in ounces of gold or silver, or in kind. When Brian Boru visited Armagh in 1004 A.D. he laid on the great altar an offering of twenty ounces of gold, equivalent to $5000 or $7000 at the present day.[157]

THE BUILDINGS:

The monastery including the whole group of monastic buildings was generally, but not always, surrounded by a strong rampart, commonly circular or elliptical, after the manner of the homesteads of the laity. The enclosure with its bounding rampart was designated in Irish by various names. When the wall was of earth it was called a *rath*, or *lios*. If surrounded by a stone wall it was known as a *caiseal* or sometimes a *cathair*.[158] Sometimes the monks located themselves in a rath or lios surrendered by a friendly chief,[159] and sometimes the monks built the enclosure themselves.[160] So much was the rampart a feature of the Irish monastery that we find it in connection with the monasteries founded by Irish monks in foreign lands. A *vallum monasterii* is mentioned by Adamnan,[161] and Columbanus utilised the walls of the old Roman *castrum* to serve as the *vallum* for his monastery at Luxeuil.[162] The monastery proper was the space enclosed by the vallum and included the church or churches, the oratories, the refectory, the kitchen, the school, the armarium—a chamber for the preservation of books and literary apparatus, sometimes a special scriptorium, the hospice or guest house, the cells for the monks, and the officinae or workshops for the smith and the carpenter.[163] Outside of the vallum were the various other indispensable buildings connected with the monastery of which the storehouse and the mill are the most important. There was usually a byre for the cows situated in convenient pasture land. If the monastery was located inland there was a fish pond; or a convenient harbour, if near the sea. The various buildings occupied different situations according to local convenience.[164]

The structure of these early monasteries was of a simple and inexpensive character. Like the early Celtic churches, they were built at first of earth, wattles, or wood. It was not until the eighth century that stone buildings began to be substituted for wooden ones, as a protection against the ravages of the Danes.[165] The simplicity and temporary character of these early foundations would account for the quickness with which monastic cities sprang up as well as for the fact that comparatively few material remains of these monastic settlements are now to be seen. They are now remembered chiefly for the great spiritual and literary heritage which they were the means of transmitting.

They were of various sizes. Those planted on barren islands off the coast of Ireland and Scotland must have been small. In each of the great monasteries of Clonard, Bangor and Clonfert there were 3000, including probably both monks and students. St. Molaise had 1,500 at Mungret, St. Gobban had 1000 and so on down to the school of St. Mobi at Glasnevin with 50. This last number, fifty, seems to have been the usual number in the smaller monastic schools.[166]

DAILY LIFE IN AN IRISH MONASTERY:

The investigations of scholars in recent years brought to light several Rules[167] which were written by early Irish saints for the direction and guidance of their monks. These Rules were frequently referred to in ancient documents, but some historians doubted their existence until their discovery set all doubts aside and furnished another proof of the trustworthiness of Irish records. By comparing these Rules with the references in the *Lives of the (Irish) Saints* [168] to the domestic and religious discipline of the monks we are able to form a tolerably correct picture of the real character of monastic life in Ireland during the period under consideration. While these Rules are neither so elaborate nor so systematic as the famous *Rule of St. Benedict*, to which they eventually gave place, yet they enable us to realize the austere simplicity of Irish monasticism.

However they may differ in details these "Rules of the Irish Saints" are in agreement as to the character of the daily work. St. Columbanus thus tersely describes the work of an Irish monastery: "Ergo quotidie jejunandum est, sicut quotidie orandum est, quotidie laborandum, quotidie est legendum."[169] Fasting and prayer, labour and study were the daily task of the monk in every Irish monastery.

FASTING:

During the whole year Wednesday and Friday were fast days in Iona and no food was taken before noon unless some "troublesome guest"[170] rendered a dispensation desirable; for charity went before sacrifice in the old Irish Canon. During Lent and Advent only one meal was allowed and that was taken in the evening.[171] Though the custom of Iona was severe, it was mildness itself as compared with that of Bangor. Only one meal was allowed the whole year round and that not eaten until evening.[172] The quality of food in Bangor was inferior to that of Iona where, as Reeves has shown, the dietary consisted of bread (sometimes made of barley), milk, fish, eggs, and probably seal's flesh. On Sundays and festivals the monks were sometimes allowed some additional luxury.[173] In Bangor, as later in Luxeuil, Anegray, and Bobbio the food apparently consisted of cabbage, pulse, flour mixed with water, a little portion of biscuit and fish.[174] Beer was sometimes allowed as a drink even by Columbanus,[175] but on the other hand St. Maelruan of Tallaght was such a strict disciplinarian that not only did he prohibit the use of beverage, but even music was forbidden. [176]

PRAYER:

A considerable portion of both day and night was given to the work of praising God. Eight times[177] a day did the monks attired in their white robes wend their way to the church for the great work of their life—the *Opus Dei*, the "Celebration of the Divine Praises." Mass was generally celebrated at an early hour each morning before the labour of the day began. The ordinary Canonical Hours were chanted in choir—Matins and Lauds generally at midnight. The Divine Office was made up of the Psalms and Lessons from the Old and New Testament. The entire Psaltery appears to have been recited during the daily office at least at certain times of the year. [178] Sometimes the choir was divided into groups which in turn chanted the Divine Praises day and night without intermission. In the monastery of Tallaght the Gospels were read in the refectory at meal times, the Gospels being taken in turn, one for each season of the year.[179]

LABOUR:

We have referred to the obligation that was placed upon all members of the monastic community to engage on some kind of manual labour.[180] Tasks requiring special skill were assigned to monks who had a natural aptitude for such work. Thus the duties of carpenter, smith, and brazier were assigned to specially qualified monks.[181] Yet even the scribes and artistic craftsmen were required to spend part of their time at ordinary manual work.[182] The word *laborare* is used in a wider sense than our term *manual labour*. The Rule of St. Columba defines the term "work" in these words: "Work is divided into three parts: viz., thine own work, and the work of the place as regards its real wants; secondly, thy share of the brethren's work; lastly, helping the neighbours by instruction, or writing, or sewing garments, or whatever labour they may be in want of."[183] Never to be idle for one moment was the monastic ideal. Accordingly Adamnan represents his hero as unable "to pass the space of one hour without applying himself either to prayer or reading, or writing, or else some manual work."[184]

STUDY:

In subsequent chapters we shall deal with the monks in their capacity as teachers and scribes. Here we shall refer briefly to their fourth task—legendum, reading or study. The study of the Sacred Scriptures was practised daily by the more learned members of the community, while the younger members learned by rote a portion of the Psalter each day until they could repeat the whole of it from memory. The story of how St. Columba when a tiny boy took up the Psalm where his tutor broke down is well known, while the numerous glosses on the Psalms and other portions of the Bible are convincing proofs of the intensive study of the Scriptures by these early monks.[185] Homilies or Lives of the Saints formed part of the sacred reading and we may reasonably suppose that the reading of the Gospels in the refectory during meal hours was a practice which was not confined to the monastery of Tallaght, nor was such reading limited to this particular time of the day. Indeed early Irish religious literature clearly points to a familiarity with the Holy Book.

OTHER PRACTICES AND CHARACTERISTICS OF IRISH MONASTIC LIFE: OBEDIENCE:

The ideal of prompt and unhesitating obedience to the commands of his superiors, so characteristic of the Irish monk, is one which cannot be understood apart from the Irish conception of Monasticism as "fighting for Christ." In all things lawful the monk yielded prompt and unquestioning obedience and was ready to go to the ends of the earth if his superior should only speak the word. The conception that the monk should be a *"miles Christi"*[186] was particularly adapted to the native temperament. To the pagan ideals of "truth, courage, and strength" were added the Christian virtues of obedience to authority, self-sacrifice, and devotion to the welfare of mankind without distinction of race or country. With such ideals they bravely encountered all privations and dangers when they undertook their "peregrinatio pro Christo." *Humility* was prized as a Christian virtue and was exemplified in many ways. The superiors though exacting prompt obedience and due respect from their monks were not tyrannical and led as strict and simple a life as the other members of the community.

There was no private property, all things were owned in common, and their wealth was limited to the means of supplying their few and simple wants. The members of the community exemplified their humility both in their demeanour towards their superiors and in dejection after sin.[187]

MORAL COURAGE:

Notwithstanding their humility these monks could, and did, show a high degree of moral courage when occasion demanded. This is shown by the action of St. Columba when he confronted the Irish King and the assembled chieftains at the Convention of Drumceat (575 A.D.).[188] Against great popular opposition he pleaded the cause of the Bardic Order and appealed for the freedom of the Irish colony in Scotland. In both cases success crowned his efforts. Still more daring was the action of St. Columbanus in his dealings with the Merovingian King, Theuderic, to whom he wrote a letter full of the bitterest reproaches and threatening to excommunicate him, if he did not immediately amend his sinful life. Thus did Columbanus draw upon himself not only the anger of the king but that of the crafty and cruel Brunechildis. Nothing daunted, however, he defied alike both their threats and violence. He adhered steadfastly to principle even though that adherence caused him to be driven from the kingdom of the Franks.[189]

SILENCE:

There was silence in the refectory during meals so that the reader could be distinctly heard, and silence was compulsory at other times also. Indeed, in their intercourse with each other the conversation of the monks was reserved at all times, but as regards their relation to society at large the objects of their system were too practical and their engagements too much characterized by common sense to impose any restraint in conversation but such as conduced to dignity and decorum.[190]

HOSPITALITY:

The monastery was usually located so as to be easily accessible to visitors for whom a special Hospice or Guest-house was provided. We have seen that when a guest arrived there was a relaxation of the fast—so strongly had the national characteristic of hospitality pervaded the monastic life.[191] Women, however, were rigidly excluded from the monastery.[192]

LOVE OF NATURE:

Another notable characteristic was the love of the monks for nature, animate and inanimate. This is shown in many ways, such as in the selection of the sites of their monasteries, and in their treatment of animals. Moreover, they often gave expression to their feelings for nature in verse, with the result that they are acknowledged to be pioneers in the field of "Nature Poetry" as well as in many other spheres of intellectual activity.[193]

Having regard to all the facts we have brought together Dr. Healy's eloquent tribute to Irish monasticism appears to be amply justified. It is worth quoting:

"Fasting and prayer, labour and study are the daily task of the monks in every monastery. How well and unselfishly that toil was performed the history of Europe tells. The monks made roads, cleared the forests, and fertilised the desert. Their monasteries in Ireland were the sites of our cities. … They preserved for us the literary treasures of antiquity; they multiplied copies of the best and newest books; they illumined them with loving care. They taught the children of rich and poor alike; … they were the greatest authors, painters, architects since the decline of the Roman Empire. They were the physicians of the poor; they served the sick in their hospitals and in their homes. And when the day's work was done in the fields or in the study, they praised God, and prayed for men who were unable or unwilling to pray for themselves. Ignorant and prejudiced men have spoken of them as an idle and useless race. They were in reality the greatest toilers, and the greatest benefactors of humanity the world has ever known."[194]

CHAPTER IV
THE RELATION OF THE IRISH MONASTIC SCHOOLS TO THE GENERAL EDUCATIONAL SITUATION (550–900 A.D.):

The wide distribution of Irish monastic schools throughout Ireland, Scotland, England, France, Belgium, Germany, and even Italy, was discussed in the previous chapter. Reference was also made to the numerous Irish missionaries who going abroad were regarded as "representative of a higher culture than was then to be found on the Continent."[195] Here we shall consider the general educational situation in Ireland with a view to determine the causes which produced results of such moment to the spread of Christianity and to restoration of learning.

During the sixth, seventh and eighth centuries the greater part of Britain and Europe was in a state of turmoil consequent on the barbarian invasion while Ireland escaped the ravages such an invasion entails. During this period of relative domestic peace Ireland was an oasis in the educational desert of Europe; then, if ever, she deserved to be styled "the school of the West, the quiet habitation of sanctity and literature."[196] In bringing about this desirable state of affairs, no doubt, the monastic schools took a leading part, but there were other contributory factors the chief of which was the lay schools whose relation to the monastic will now be touched upon very briefly. We shall also endeavour to determine the extent to which education prevailed among the different classes of society—and finally we shall discuss the question of the admission of foreign students to Irish monastic schools.

DUAL SYSTEM OF SCHOOLS:

The schools of ancient Ireland were of two classes, lay and ecclesiastical. The ecclesiastical or monastic schools as we have seen were of Christian origin, and were conducted by monks. The lay, or secular, schools existed from a period of unknown antiquity, and in pagan times were taught by druids. The monastic schools were celebrated all over Europe during the Middle Ages: the lay schools though playing an important part in spreading learning at home are not so well known.

These two classes of schools are quite distinct all through the literary history of Ireland, and without conflicting with each other worked contemporaneously from the sixth to the nineteenth century.[197]

LAY SCHOOLS:

As we are mainly interested in the monastic schools we shall deal with the lay schools only so far as is necessary to explain the general educational situation in Ireland during the period we have chosen. Originally pagan and taught by druids these lay schools held their ground after the general spread of the new faith, but were now taught by Christian *ollamhna* or doctors, laymen who took the place of the druid teachers of earlier times. [198]

The aim of these schools at first was apparently to prepare a limited number of men as *brehons* or judges, and *filí* or poets, and *senachidhe* or historians. In very early times the same man performed two or more of these offices. In later times there was a tendency to specialization. A lay college generally comprised three distinct schools. We are told that Cormac MacAirt, King of Ireland (254–277 A.D.) founded three schools, one for the study of Military Science, one for Law and one for General Literature.[199] It would appear that schools of this last type developed into the "Bardic Schools" in which were taught poetry, history, and vernacular literature in general. The law schools and military schools were evidently exclusively professional, whereas the "Bardic Schools" were attended by those seeking admission to the Bardic Order and others desiring a liberal education.[200]

RE-ORGANIZATION OF BARDIC SCHOOLS:

The members of Bardic Order became so numerous and exacting in their demands as to arouse widespread dissatisfaction with the result that the complete abolition of the Order was contemplated. Owing to the timely intervention of St. Columba reform was substituted for abolition. At the Convention of Drum-Ceata in 573 A.D. St. Columba who had received part of his own education in a Bardic School pleaded the cause of the bards with such success that the whole system of public secular education was reorganized. The scheme was devised by the chief poet (*ard-ollamh*) of Ireland, Dallan Forgaill. There was to be a chief school or college for each of the five provinces; and under these were several smaller schools, one for each *tuath* or district. They were all endowed with lands and all those persons who needed it received free education in them. The heads of these schools were *ollamhna* doctors of literature and poetry, and were all laymen. [201]

There was now a great tendency towards specialization. Many schools became noted for the excellency of their teaching in particular branches of learning according to the individual tastes or bent of mind of the teachers or the traditions of the several schools. These subjects whether Law, History, Antiquities, Poetry, etc. were commonly taught by the same family for generations.[202]

EDUCATION OF LAYMEN:

It has sometimes been asserted that in early times learning in Ireland was confined to ecclesiastics, but this assertion is quite erroneous. We have shown that there were numerous facilities afforded laymen both for a professional and a general education. Nearly all the professional men, physicians, lawyers (Brehons), poets, builders, and historians were laymen; lay tutors were employed to teach princes; and in fact laymen played a very important part in the diffusion of knowledge and in building up that character for learning that rendered Ireland famous in former times.[203] A glance through Ware's *Irish Writers*, or O'Reilly's *Irish Writers*, or Hyde's *Literary History of Ireland* or Miss Hull's *Text Book of Irish Literature* is enough to convince the most sceptical on this point.[204]

RELATION OF THE LAY SCHOOL TO
THE MONASTIC SCHOOL:

Though differing in aim, both the lay school and the monastic school were so closely related to the social system that there does not appear to have been any actual antagonism between them. They were to a large extent complementary. As an instance of the friendly relations which obtained between the ecclesiastics and the lay school we might cite the fact, already referred to, that St. Columba pleaded the cause of the bards. St. Columba himself had practical experience of the bards as teachers. We are told that after he had spent some years at the monastic school of Finnian of Movilla and having been ordained deacon he placed himself under the instruction of an aged bard called Gemman.[205] Nor did his monks in the severe and pious solitude of Iona lose their love for their national poetry. On one occasion it is recorded they inquired from the saint why he did not ask an Irish poet who visited Iona to recite a poem for them after the sermon—a question that did not scandalize the saint in the least.[206] We know also that much of the pagan literature was preserved by monastic scribes, and some of the finest Old Irish poems that have been discovered were written by monks on the margin of MSS. they were copying.[207] These examples are given for the purpose of removing a false impression that there was a clear cut line of demarcation between the study of native and classical literature.

As a learned French Celticist writes: "On aurait tort de croire qu'en Irelande il y eût entre les savants addonés aux lettres classiques où à la théologie, alors leurs inseparable associée, — et les gens des lettres voués à la culture de la littérature nationale, la ligne de séparation presque infranchissable qu'on remarque pendant le moyen âge sur le continent."[208]

On the other hand many laymen attended Monastic schools at some period of their lives not only to get religious instruction but to get a wider general education.[209] Besides laymen were sometimes professors in the monastic schools, and even occupied the important position of Fer-leighinn or Principal of a monastic school, for example Flann Mainistrech (d. 1056 A.D.), a layman and the most learned scholar in Ireland of his time, was appointed Fer-leighinn of Monasterboice. About a century earlier the lay ollamh, Mac Cosse, held a similar position in the great school of Ros-Ailithir, now Ros Carbery, in Cork.[210]

Owing to the increasing popularity of the monastic schools and the appointment of laymen as professors in monastic schools there was a tendency to introduce into the Bardic school some of the subjects which attracted lay students to monastic schools. St. Bricin's College at Tomregan (recte Tuaim Drecain) near Ballyconnel in Cavan, founded in the seventh century, though having an ecclesiastic for Principal was typical of the lay schools. It had one school for law, one for classics, and one for poetry and general Gaelic learning. Each school was under a special *druimcli*, or head professor,[211] corresponding apparently to a Dean in a modern university.

HOME EDUCATION AND FOSTERAGE:

Thus far we have dealt with literary and professional education. It remains to add a few words in regard to what may be called home education. This education was partly literary and partly technical in nature, and differed according to the age, sex, and social position of the child.

In addition to the usual literary education the sons of the chiefs were instructed in archery, swimming, and chess-playing,[212] while the daughters were taught sewing, cutting-out and embroidery. The sons of chiefs were also taught horsemanship. The children of the wealthy class were often put to fosterage and the foster father was held responsible for the instruction in these branches for neglect of which he was punished by a fine of two-thirds the fosterage fee. The Brehon Law clearly defines the relation between the teacher and pupil in the following words:

"The social position that is considered between the foster-pupil and his foster-father is that the latter is to instruct him without reserve, and to prepare him for his degree, and to chastise him without severity; to feed and to clothe him while he is learning his lawful profession unless he obtains it (food and clothing) from another person. On the other hand, the foster son is to assist his tutor in poverty, and support his old age, and to give him the honour price of the degree for which he is being prepared, and all the gains of his art while he is earning it, and the first earning of his art after he has left the house of his tutor; and moreover the literary foster father has power of judgment and proof and witnesses upon his foster son as the father has upon his son."[213]

In the case of children who were put to fosterage the parents were apparently left to their own discretion as to the training of their children in their own homes. In such a case the instruction was of the more or less technical type that all must master to a greater or less extent in order to discharge the ordinary duties of life.[214]

Notwithstanding the facilities afforded by the numerous lay and monastic schools the great body of the people were probably neither able to read or write, yet they were not uneducated. They had an education of another kind, reciting poetry, historical tales, and legends, or listening to recitation in which all took delight. In every hamlet there was one or more amateur reciters. This practice of listening to the recitation of stories and poems was then as general as the reading of newspapers and story-books is at the present day.[215] Anyone acquainted with the social life of the Irish-speaking peasantry even in modern Ireland and has listened to a story told, or poem recited, by a *seanchaidhe* (raconteur) will realise that this was true education, a real exercise for the intellect and a refined source of enjoyment. Taking education then in the broad sense we see that the great body of the Irish people in these early times were really educated.

EDUCATION OF WOMEN:

We have ample evidence that education in ancient Ireland was not confined to men. As we have already seen, the Brehon Laws made provision for the education of girls as well as for that of boys. In a convent established by St. Brigid (d. 525 A.D.) at Kildare we are told that St. Mel was employed to instruct herself and her nurse,[216] and the history of that school would lead us to infer that it compared not unfavourably with some of the great monastic schools. St. Brendan of Clonfert (d. 577 A.D.) when a child about one year old was placed in fosterage in the convent of St. Ita at Killeedy, Co. Limerick, where he remained for five years. This young saint always looked upon St. Ita as his foster mother and often had listened to her counsels.[217] On one occasion she advised him not to study with women lest some evilly disposed person might revile him.[218] We may safely infer from this that it was not unusual for young children to receive the rudiments of education from the nuns, but that by the time they reached the age of six or more probably seven years[219] they were sent to the monastic school. Moreover, St. Ita's words of advice clearly suggest that education was provided for girls but that except in the case of children of pre-adolescent age she was decidedly opposed to co-education. Unlike St. Brendan and some other saints, St. Columbanus was not put to fosterage and his childhood's days were spent in his father's home under his mother's care.[220] His latest and best biographer informs us that he received his earliest literary education from an elderly lady who lived near his parent's home.[221] One of the First Order of Saints named Mugint founded a school in Scotland to which girls as well as boys were admitted.[222] It is evident likewise that the Irish missionaries in Northumbria did much for the education of women. Among the more noteworthy convents or monasteries for women that owe their origin to Irish missionaries were St. Bees, Coldingham, Streanshalch or Whitby which are all referred to by Bede.[223] It was in this last-named monastery and by the enlightened patronage of Abbess Hilda that the earliest Anglo-Saxon poet, Caedmon, was encouraged in his efforts.[224] That women were sometimes accomplished scribes is quite probable. In an old record we are informed that in the sixth century King Branduff's mother had a writing style (delg graiph), so that she must have practised writing on waxen tablets,[225] this being spoken of in old MSS. as a common practice among ladies.[226]

There is not sufficient evidence to justify the assertion that girls were admitted as students to monastic schools, though we read that one of the daughters of the King of Cualann was sent to Clonard to learn to read her Psalms (in Latin),[227] and Plummer thinks that women taught in this school.[228] Probably there was a separate school for women. From what we know of the Second Order of Saints to which St. Finnian, the founder of Clonard, belonged we cannot believe that co-education would be likely to receive any sanction as a desirable practice in a monastic school. On the other hand, with Mugint and the other saints of the First Order such a practice may possibly have been quite usual; for "strong in faith they feared not the breath of temptation."[229]

Many other instances of educational facilities for women might be adduced, but enough has been said to prove the position for which we have been contending, namely, that though education was not universal nor compulsory there was ample facilities for all to acquire a liberal education. That a very large proportion of both sexes availed themselves of this privilege there can be no reasonable doubt.

FOREIGN STUDENTS IN IRELAND:

The fame of the Irish monastic schools of the seventh, eighth and ninth centuries attracted a large number of students from foreign lands. To these the Irish monks extended freely the benefits of education which during this period were not available in their own less favoured lands.

The *Felire of Aengus* [230] which according to linguistic and other internal evidence was written as early as the seventh century[231] mentions various nationalities who have died in Ireland: Romans, Gauls, sometimes called Franks, monks of Egypt, and Saxons (more correctly Angles). The well-known stone inscription "VII Romani" in the churchyard of St. Brecan in Arranmore[232] testifies to this day of presence of Romans. It is also known that in times of persecution Egyptian monks fled to Ireland.[233] In this same calendar of Aengus mention is made of seven Egyptian monks who died in one place. Scattered through the *Lives of Irish Saints* there are innumerable passages recording the arrival and departure of foreign pilgrims or students, or noting their residence or death. Thus we hear of Britons, including a British bishop, at Clonfert; of British monks at Rahen, Lynally, Taghmon, Clonard, Ferns, and Tallaght; of a British priest at Hare Island in Lough Ree; of British "peregrini" at Tullach Bennan. We even know the names of many British saints who studied or resided in Ireland: Cadoc under St. Mocuda at Lismore, Gildas, Carantoc, Cybi, Petroc, and Sampson.[234] Aldhelm, bishop of Shereboree (705–707 A.D.) in a letter to Eadfrid, bishop of Lindisfarne, states that "fleet loads" of Angles went to Ireland.[235] A passage in Bede corroborates Aldhelm's testimony. Speaking of the ravages of the Yellow Plague in 664 A.D. Bede says: "This pestilence did no less harm in the island of Ireland. Many of the nobility and of the lower ranks of the English nation were there at the time who in the days of the Bishops Finan (651–661) and Colman (661–664), forsaking their native island retired thither either for the sake of divine studies, or a more continent life: and some of them presently devoted themselves to monastic life; others chose rather to apply themselves to study, going from one master's cell to another. The Scots willingly received them all, and took care to supply them with food as well as to furnish them with books to read and their teaching all gratis."[236] The bishop Finan and Colman who are referred to by Bede were respectively the second and third abbots of Lindisfarne.

After the Synod of Whitby (644 A.D.) Colman and his English adherents who refused to adopt the Roman usage with regard to the date of Easter and the form of tonsure retired to a small island called Inisbofinn off the coast of Mayo and there founded a monastery about 667 A.D. A little later

Colman founded another monastery on the mainland which he placed in charge of his English companions and disciples. As late as 730 A.D. at least this monastery was occupied by English monks and was named by the Irish "Mayo of the Saxons."[237] We know too that one of the divisions of Armagh was called "Trian Saxon" or the Saxon's Third from the great number of English students inhabiting it, and we learn incidentally that in the eighth century seven streets in a town called Kilbally near Rahen in King's Co. were wholly occupied by Galls, or foreigners.[238]

Among the foreign students there were sometimes princes. Of the more illustrious of these we may mention Oswald (d. 642) and Ailfrid (d. 704), kings of Northumbria, and Dagobert II. (d. 679) king of France, all of whom were educated in Ireland. Owing to one of those wars so common in England in the seventh century Oswald, son of King Ethelfrid of Northumbria, had to seek refuge in Ireland when he was fifteen years old. He was educated in a monastery and became a Christian. On regaining his kingdom he sought the aid of the monks of Iona to convert his heathen subjects. In 635 A.D. St. Aidan arrived in Northumbria and founded a monastery on the island of Lindisfarne which was destined to become the Iona of the North of England. [239] Ailfrid, another Northumbria king, spent his schooldays in Ireland. While there he was called the Irish Flann Fina (literally Fina's Flann) from his mother Fina who was an Irish princess. There is still extant a very ancient Irish poem[240] which he composed in praise of Ireland. He would appear to have got a very good education; for Aldhelm in dedicating to him an epistle on Latin prosody congratulates him on having been educated in Ireland. [241] After the death of King Sigibert his little son, who eventually became Dagobert II., was brought by Didon, bishop of Pointers, to Ireland to be educated. This was done at the command of Grimoald, Mayor of the Palace. [242] The greatest of English missionaries, Wilibrord (657–739) was educated in Ireland where he spent thirteen years. With twelve companions, some of them Irish, and other English whom he selected from the Irish schools, he set sail for Friesland and converted that country to the Christian faith.[243] As Alcuin says so tersely, Britain gave him birth but Ireland reared and educated him. ("Quem tibi iam genuit fecunda Britannia mater doctaque nutrivit studiis sed Hibernia sacris.")[244] Bede mentions other Anglo-Saxon missionaries who in addition to Wilibrord received their training in Irish schools; of these the most familiar names are Victbert and Hewald.[245] Agilbert, a native of Gaul, after spending some time in Ireland studying the Scriptures, was appointed bishop of the West Saxons in 650 A.D. and later occupied the episcopal see of Paris.[246] Other distinguished students were the Angles, Chad and Egbert. Bede tells us that Egbert spent a long time in exile in Ireland studying the Scriptures.[247] Apparently the prestige of the

Irish schools continued to draw many students from England even after the establishment of schools in their own country; for we find Aldhelm (d. 709 A.D.) writing in a somewhat bitter mood to three young men who had just returned from the Irish schools: "Why does Ireland pride herself on such a priority that such numbers of students look there from England, as if upon this fruitful soil there were not abundance of *Argivi didasculi* (or Greek masters), to be found fully capable of solving the deepest problems of religion and satisfying the most ambitious of students."[248] Zimmer looks upon the reluctance of Aldhelm to acknowledge the superiority of the Irish monastic schools as an additional testimony in their favour.[249]

There are some grounds for believing that Alcuin whose name is intimately connected with the Carolingian revival of learning studied in Ireland, probably in Clonmacnoise. Meyer,[250] Joyce,[251] and Healy,[252] do not hesitate to claim him as a student of Clonmacnoise. Turner[253] thinks it more probable that he was a student of the school of York (in which case he came under Irish as well as Roman influence[254]) but regards him as representative of Irish rather than English scholarship. The opinion that Alcuin studied at Clonmacnoise is based on a letter[255] which is evidently one of a series written by Alcuin to Colchu (d. 792 A.D.), Fer-leighinn, or Headmaster of the school of Clonmacnoise. This Colchu was a very distinguished scholar and teacher. There is no evidence that he ever left Ireland, but his name was well known on the Continent. The general opinion of his contemporaries was that "no one in any age or any country was equal to him in learning, or equal to him in sanctity."[256] In this letter, which is of a very cordial nature, Alcuin styles Colchu his holy father and speaks of himself as his son. The writer complains that for some time past he was not deemed worthy to receive any of those letters so precious in his sight, and concludes by saying he is sending a messenger with presents from himself and King Charles (Charlemagne) to Clonmacnoise and other Irish monasteries.[257] Dr. Healy points out that some of these gifts are of such a nature as to suggest that Alcuin had a personal knowledge of the needs of Irish monasteries.[258]

No doubt, further research would reveal many other instances of foreign students who sought in Ireland and there were freely given the education which was not available in their own lands. In summarising the conclusions which we believe are justified by the facts presented in this chapter we would say:

1. That both the monastic schools and the bardic schools were so intimately connected with the native Irish social system that they were not antagonistic but rather complementary to each other.

2. That these two classes of schools exerted a mutual influence on each other: the aim of the monastic schools was frankly religious, yet owing to the influence of the bardic schools vernacular learning was not neglected; moreover, as we shall see later, the monks were led for a variety of reasons to study the writings of the classical authors; on the other hand, the bardic schools though mainly devoted to the cultivation of native learning followed the example of the monastic schools in introducing classical learning, thus widening their own curriculum.

3. That with the abundant facilities thus afforded there was ample opportunity for everyone who so desired to acquire liberal education in either a lay or ecclesiastical school.

4. That though education was not universal nor compulsory, the great body of the people without distinction of class or sex was not uneducated.

5. That the educational advantages enjoyed by the Irish in their native land were as freely extended to others irrespective of race or country.

6. That the educational influence of the Irish monastic schools reached Britain and the Continent in two ways: first, numerous students from foreign countries who studied in the schools of Ireland would on returning to their own country naturally endeavour to transmit the culture they had acquired during their residence in Ireland; secondly, still more important was the influence of the numerous bands of Irish missionaries who, as we have shown, established monasteries all over Western Europe and whose love of learning was equalled only by their zeal for Christianity.

CHAPTER V
CENTRES OF INTELLECTUAL LIFE
IN IRISH MONASTERIES

In an Irish monastic school, as in the case of every other school, the most important centre of intellectual life was the class-room. Unlike our modern schools, however, these schools had to produce their own text-books. This work was carried on in a special room called the scriptorium. The work of the scriptorium was not limited to the production of text-books. Often valuable books of more permanent interest were written in the scriptorium and stored for reference in a special room, the library. In this way copies of many of the most treasured books of antiquity have been preserved for posterity. Indeed the educational work of the scriptorium and the library was scarcely less important than that of the class-room, or school proper. These three centres of intellectual life were closely related to each other, but each is sufficiently important to warrant a separate treatment.

THE SCHOOL:

In the last chapter we stated that the *aim* of the monastic school was frankly religious. In our next chapter we hope to prove that in practice this did not necessarily mean a narrow *curriculum*. Here we shall briefly state that the particulars we have been able to glean on a miscellaneous collection of topics are of some interest to the educationist. The data are so few on each topic that the treatment is necessarily somewhat disconnected. In general these topics refer to school age, accommodation of students, school buildings, methods of teaching and pedagogical principles so far as they are revealed in the meagre materials to hand.

Seven years was the age at which it was thought schooling should begin. [259] We do not know exactly what provision was made for young boys of this tender age, but we know that in case of the older students a few resided in the school itself, so it is possible that the younger children also resided in the school or in the houses of the teachers. Many of the students lived in the houses of people in the neighbourhood of the school, but the majority lived in huts which they built for themselves near the school. Where the school was a large one these huts were arranged in streets.[260] The poorer students lived in houses with the richer ones whom they waited upon and served, receiving in return food, clothing, and other necessities. Some even chose to live in this matter, not through poverty but through a self-imposed penance.[261]

There were no spacious lecture halls; the master taught and lectured and the pupils studied very much in the open air, when weather permitted.[262] Judging by the large number of monks in every monastery and recalling the fact that teaching was regarded as a most meritorious form of labour, we are inclined to think that there was a great deal of individual teaching, or at least teaching in small groups, especially when the weather was unfavourable for outdoor lectures. This conjecture derives some support from Bede, who informs us that of the Anglo-Saxons who went to Ireland many of them passed from one master's cell to another for instruction.[263]

METHODS OF TEACHING:

In teaching *reading* it was usual to begin with the *Alphabet*. St. Columba's first alphabet was written or impressed upon a cake which he afterwards ate as he played by the side of a stream near his tutor's home.[264] Sometimes the alphabet was engraved upon a large stone.[265] The Psalms in Latin seem to have been the earliest subject of instruction.[266] As we have seen these were learned by rote, but judging by the numerous glosses and annotations[267] thereon it is almost certain that the teachers were not satisfied with mere repetition but explained the meaning thoroughly.

It may seem strange that the reading of Latin should be taught before the reading of the vernacular. The explanation is simple. The Irish alphabet is based on the Latin (as are the alphabets of most European languages) and consequently suits the phonetic system of the Irish language less perfectly than it does the Latin. Having learned the alphabet the reading of Latin is comparatively easy even for young students. At a later stage when the reading of the vernacular was introduced progress was no doubt rapid since the student had merely to associate the written symbols with sounds that were familiar to him.

The next stage was to teach writing. The letters were formed on a waxen tablet (*polaire* in Irish) with a pointed metal style (*graib*).[268] One of these old-time tablets is now in the National Museum, Dublin.[269] The writing on it is in Latin, apparently a pupil's class notes.

Joyce thinks that there were no elementary books for teaching Latin and that the pupil had to face the difficulties of the language in a rough and ready manner, beginning right away at the author.[270] With this view we do not agree. There are still extant numerous vocabularies, paradigms, treatises on declensions, and several copies of Priscian's grammatical tract all in the style of writing practised by Irish scribes. In such works we have clear evidence of preparations made to smooth the path for beginners. Our view is in harmony with the maxim laid down in the eighth century gloss: "It is the custom with good teachers (dagforcitlidib) to praise the understanding of their pupils that *they may love what they hear*."[271] There is a similar reminder in another eighth century gloss.[272] This quotation is interesting as showing that oral teaching was practised, that good teaching was appreciated, that the methods of good teachers were commended for imitation and further that the learning process was to be as pleasant as possible. It would be a mistake to imagine that the desire to make learning attractive began and ended with the carving of alphabets on cakes. In the same connection we may refer to the practice of many eminent teachers who were wont to compose educational poems embodying the leading facts of history and other branches of instruction. A considerable number of compositions in old Irish MSS. are of this class. These poems were explained and commented upon by their authors and learned by rote by the pupils. Flann of Monasterboice followed this plan and we still have several of his educational poems on historical subjects.[273]

There is a curious geographical poem[274] forming a sort of text-book on general geography which was used in the school of Ros-Ailithir in Cork of which the author MacCosse was Principal (Fer-leighinn). This poem contained practically all that was then known of the principal countries of the world. It was written about the beginning of the tenth century. The tenth century map of the world drawn in England for an Anglo-Saxon is supposed to have been the work of an Irish artist.[275] Although inaccurate in many particulars this map is historically interesting as showing the state of geographical knowledge at this time.

In teaching Greek the Irish monks used the *Nermeneumata* of the Pseudo-Dositheus, the work of Macrobius *De Differentiis et Societatibus Graeci Latinique Verbi*, Latin glosses and interlinear versions.[276] With regard to the Pseudo-Dositheus and the book of Macrobius, Traube believes that were it not for the fact that these books were used by the Irish in teaching Greek both would have been lost to the afterworld. Mrs. Concannon conjectures that the earliest teachers of Latin brought with them to Ireland the third century *Disticha Catonis* and used them as materials for teaching as well as for moral instruction.[277] The many copies of Priscian with numerous glosses thereon would suggest that this work was extensively used in Irish monastic schools. Traube has shown conclusively that the St. Gall copy of Priscian was written by some friends of Sedulius (of Liège) and supposes it was copied in some Irish monastery about the beginning of the ninth century and brought by Irishmen to the Continent.[278] Indeed, the glosses everywhere furnish objective proofs that the Irish monks were skilled practical teachers as well as accomplished classical scholars. In all these interlinear and marginal notes so abundant in the MSS. of the Old Irish period (prior to 900 A.D.) we see clear evidence of preparation for the work of teaching.

It is worthy of note that in the earlier stages of instruction the pupil was encouraged to ask questions about the difficulties which he encountered and the tutor was expected to explain everything that was obscure to the learner. At a later stage the learner was questioned to test whether he had grasped the meaning of what he read, and to raise difficulties which he was required to explain.[279] In fact the instruction would seem to have been thorough and in many respects was at least equal in efficiency, if not in technique, to that imparted in many of our modern schools. We are told that it was the special merit of the tutor who obtained the degree known as *Sruth-do-aill* that "he was able to modify his instruction to the complexion of the information in mercy to the people who were unable to follow the instruction of a teacher of higher degree. In other words he was able to make hard things easy to weak students who might get frightened in the presence of the formidable scholar."[280] This would show that the question of "individual differences" was a live one in pedagogical circles in those days and that a genuine attempt was made to solve it. When we come in a later chapter to discuss the characteristics of the groups of figures represented on the sculptured crosses we shall see that the value of "visual instruction" was appreciated.

THE SCRIPTORIUM:

The function of the scriptorium was to supply text-books for the school, service books for the church and monastic community, and works of a more general and ambitious nature for the library. Our knowledge of the internal life of the scriptorium is unfortunately very limited and is deduced almost entirely from an examination of the MSS. produced therein. It would seem that the scriptorium was not unlike a modern school-room in some respects. In silence the younger members of the monastic community and other students sat there writing out and multiplying books, sometimes from dictation, sometimes by copying. An invigilator sat there also to preserve silence and to act as task master. On the margins of the MSS. we sometimes find short fragmentary notes devoid of literary value, but of deep human interest as showing that unregenerate human nature had its opportunities even in a monastic scriptorium as much as in a modern school-room. These notes[281] are supposed to be fragments of conversations carried on *sotto voce* to evade the rule of silence and doubtlessly notes were scribbled surreptitiously to companions. Though all too few these vivid human touches add not a little to our knowledge of student life in those far off days.

The scribes made all the *writing materials*: tablets, vellum, ink, pens. We have shown that *wax tablets* were used in teaching writing. They were also used in teaching reading, and for such temporary purposes as taking notes of a sermon or lecture.[282] Adamnan writing in the seventh century mentions that he inscribed certain writings first on wax tablets and afterwards on vellum.[283] For memoranda a *slate and pencil* were also used, as we learn from the story of Cinnfaela the Learned. When he was at the school of Tuaim Drecain, now Tom Regan in Co. Cavan, he wrote down roughly on slates what he heard during the day, but at night he transferred the entries into a vellum book.[284] These tablets were made of long strips of wood and covered with beeswax. In shape they were sometimes like short swords.

The schools prepared their own vellum or parchment from the skins of goats, sheep, and calves. This parchment was usually finely polished, but sometimes it was hard and not well cleaned. The parchment prepared by the Irish scribes was much thicker than that used by the French from the seventh to the tenth century: thus we have an additional means whereby we can identify Irish MSS. on the Continent.[285]

The ink was made of carbon. It has been found to resist all the chemical tests for iron. The blackness of the ink even at the present day is quite remarkable. The writing of the *Book of Armagh*, for instance, is as black as if it were written yesterday.[286]

The ink was very likely made of lampblack, or possibly of fish bone black.[287] When we come to describe the illuminated MSS. which remain to attest the artistic skill of the monastic scribes we shall see that not only were they experts at making a superior quality of ink but, what is still more remarkable, they manufactured a large variety of pigments which even at the present day have lost little of their original brilliancy after a lapse of one thousand years.

PENS:

The beauty, neatness, and perfect uniformity of the handwriting in old Irish MSS. have led some antiquarians to express an opinion that the scribes used metal pens; but such an opinion is quite untenable. Keller has shown that the pens were made from the quills of geese, swans, crows, and other birds.[288] This is also the opinion of Miss Stokes.[289] One of the pictures in the *Book of Kells* confirms this view. This is a picture representing St.

John the Evangelist engaged in writing the Gospel. He holds a pen in his hand the feather of which can be clearly detected.[290] The inkstand is also represented by a slender conical cup fastened to the corner of the chair on which he is sitting or upon a stick stuck in the ground.

The old scribes sometimes wrote with the book resting upon the knees using a flat board for support. But when writing became more elaborate and ornamental a desk was used and, if necessary, a maulstick to support the wrist.[291]

THE SCRIBE:

In almost every monastery there was at least one especially expert scribe who was selected partly because of his scholarship, and partly because of his skill in penmanship. Outside of the time set apart for religious exercises the scribe devoted almost his whole time to the work of copying and multiplying books. At a time when there were no printed books we can easily imagine the important part played by the scribe in the educational life of the monastery.

Not only did the scribes produce the necessary books for class use, but by their indefatigable industry they preserved those valuable relics of the past—a large mass of historical records and numerous specimens of the literature of ancient times. To copy a book was considered a highly meritorious work, especially if it were a part of the Scriptures, or any other book on sacred or devotional subjects.[292] The scribe was therefore highly honoured. The Brehon Laws prescribed the same penalty for the murder of a scribe as for that of an abbot or bishop and, as we pointed out,[293] the Annals in recording the death of a man otherwise learned or eminent whether bishop, abbot, priest, or lay professor considered it an enhancement of his dignity to add that he was an excellent scribe, *scribhneoir tocchaidhe*. The *Four Masters* record the obits of 61 eminent scribes before the year 900 A.D. of whom 40 lived between 700 and 800 A.D. One has only to glance at some of the MSS. that have come down to us to realise what excellent penmen these ancient scribes were. Such skill could only be acquired after years of careful training. As will be shown later the scribe was an accomplished artist as well as an expert penman.

IRISH SCRIPT:

The Irish style of writing played an important part in development not only of the modern Irish hand, but of the style of writing practised for centuries in England and to some extent on the Continent also, hence the necessity of giving a brief account of its history. There is little doubt that Ireland modelled her national script on the Roman half-uncial hand, but, as Reeves has pointed out, the Greek and Roman letters as written by the Irish scribes mutually affected each other and gave the Irish alphabet, especially in the capitals that peculiar form which distinguishes it from all others.[294] The Roman half-uncial hand, however, was the basis from which the characteristic Irish had developed. In the words of a recognised authority,[295] "The Irish scribe adopted the Roman half-uncial script and then with his own innate sense of beauty of form he produced from it the handsome literary hand which culminated in the native half-uncial writing as seen in perfection in the *Book of Kells* and contemporary MSS. of the latter part of the seventh century. But the round half-uncial hand thus formed was too elaborate for the ordinary uses of life. It was necessary to produce a script that would serve all the duties of a current hand. Therefore, taking the Roman half-uncial hand the Irish scribe adapted it to commoner uses, and writing the letters more negligently he evolved the compact, pointed minuscule hand which became the current form of handwriting of the country and which again in its turn was in the course of time moulded into the book hand which superseded the half-uncial." The absence of an extraneous influence was an important factor in aiding the development of a strongly characteristic national hand which ran its uninterrupted course down to the late Middle Ages and is still retained with slight variations in the writing of Modern Irish. The high degree of cultivation of Irish writing did not result from the genius of single individuals, but from the emulation of various schools of writing and the improvements of several generations. "There is not a single letter in the entire alphabet which does not give evidence both in the general form and in its minutest parts of the sound judgment and taste of the penman."[296]

IRISH HAND ABROAD:

Not only did the Irish perfect this script in the schools of their native land, but they carried it with them when they went abroad and taught it in the schools which they founded in foreign countries. Owing to the fact that the Irish schools kept up the tradition of Greek and Latin learning, philologists and palaeographers have studied the development of Irish writing very carefully with a view to determining the dates of classical MSS. which were transcribed by Irish monks or their pupils. The most important of these studies are those made by Keller[297] and Lindsey.[298] The work of these scholars has placed the question of the influence of the Irish style of writing beyond dispute.

"England borrowed it *en bloc*; and in the Early Middle Ages the Irish missionaries who spread over the continent of Europe and who became the founders of religious houses carried their native script with them and taught it to their pupils. Thus in such centres as Luxeuil in France, Würzburg in Germany, St. Gall in Switzerland, and Bobbio in Italy, Irish writing flourished and MSS. in the Irish hand multiplied. At first there was no difference between the writing in these MSS. and that in the Irish codices actually written in Ireland. But as might be expected the script thus employed in isolated foreign places gradually deteriorated as the bonds with the native hand relaxed and the Irish monks died off."[299] From these MSS. written in the characteristic Irish script we are able to form some idea, though an inadequate one, of the magnitude and importance of the work done by the Irish monks in preserving the ancient classics. Moreover, in addition to those MSS. described as *Scottice Scripta* by continental librarians, Zimmer has shown that many of the MSS. ostensibly the work of the continental scholars are in reality the work of Irish monks.[300] The explanation is that those monks who studied on the Continent tried as far as possible to accustom themselves to the forms of the letters used by continental scholars. For instance, this is the case of all the documents written by Moengal at St. Gall between the years 853–860 A.D.[301]

LIBRARIES:

An important feature of every monastic school was the library, or *tech screptra*, as it is styled in the older Irish MSS. When we recall the fame of these schools, the needs of the students, and the number of scribes whose business it was to cater to these needs we might reasonably infer that these libraries were provided with text-books and with books for general reading. These libraries differed widely from our modern libraries. There were no shelves for rows of books, but there was another arrangement which was more suitable for the type of book then in use. The books were kept in satchels hung on pegs or racks round the room. Each satchel containing one or more volumes was labelled on the outside. The satchels were of embossed leather beautifully adorned with designs of interlaced ornament so common in Irish art. Many specimens of these satchels are on view in the National Museum, Dublin, and there is one in Corpus Christi College, Oxford.[302] These satchels were also used when carrying a book from place to place.

The book itself was of parchment. Manuscripts which were greatly valued were usually kept in elaborately embossed leather covers of which two are still preserved, namely, the cover of the *Book of Armagh*,[303] and that of the Shrine of St. Maidoc.[304]

Books abounded in Ireland when the Danes made their appearance there about the end of the eighth century; hence the pride with which the old writers referred to "the hosts of the books of Erin." But with the first Danish incursions began an era of burning and pillaging the monasteries and consequently a woeful destruction of MSS., the records of the ancient learning. The special fury of the invaders appears to have been directed against books, monasteries, and monuments of religion. All the books they could lay hands upon they either burned or "drowned" by throwing them into the nearest river, or lake. For two centuries this wanton destruction continued, and ceased only when the Danes were finally crushed at the Battle of Clontarf in 1014 A.D.[305]

During the Danish period missionaries and scholars who went abroad carried with them great numbers of MSS. As a result of the exportation as well as of the destruction of MSS. we can merely conjecture as to the extent and value of the books in a library attached to a great Irish monastic school during the period covered by our investigation. Fortunately, however, we are able to describe the contents of the libraries of the Irish establishment of St. Gall in Switzerland, and Bobbio in Italy, and this may serve to give us some idea of the wealth of material the Irish libraries once possessed, but most of it is now irreparably lost.

A catalogue of the Bobbio library was made between the years 967–972 A.D. It is attributed to the Abbot Gerbert who afterwards became Pope Silvester II.[306] At this time the library contained about 700 volumes,[307] of which 479 had been acquired gradually from various unstated sources, and over 220 had been presented by scholars who are named with the list of books they had given,[308] 43 having been a donation from the famous Irish monk Dungal who presided over the school of Pavia.[309] This catalogue itself is strong objective evidence for the claim we are making that the classical authors were read. The list of MSS. shows that both Greek and Latin classics, were well represented. Among others we find works by the following authors: Terence, Lucretius, Virgil, Ovid, Lucian, Martial, Juvenal, Claudian, Cicero, Seneca, and the Elder Pliny;[310] also Persius, Flaccus, Horace, Demosthenes, and Aristotle.[311]

The greater part of the Bobbio collection has been dispersed through the libraries of Rome, Milan, Naples, and Vienna.[312] It is practically certain that the Ambrosian palimpsest of Plautus and those of several of Cicero's orations and of the letters of Fronto discovered in the Ambrosian Library (Milan) early in the ninth century all came from the monastery founded by the Irish monk of Bobbio.[313] Among other MSS. which once belonged to Bobbio may be mentioned fragments of Symmachus (in Milan) and the Theodosian Code (formerly in Turin), Scholia on Cicero (v. century) MSS. of St. Luke (v.–vi. cent.), St. Severinus (vi. cent.), Josephus (vi.–vii.), Gregory's Dialogue (c. 750) and St. Isadore's (before 840). Last but not least we must mention the "Muratori Fragment" (viii. cent., or earlier), the earliest extant list of Books of the New Testament.[314]

St. Agilius (St. Aile), a pupil of St. Columbanus the founder of Bobbio, was first abbot of the monastery founded at Resbacus (Rébais, east of Paris) in 634 A.D.[315] The MSS. copied there included the works of Terence, Cicero, Virgil, Horace, Donatus, Priscian and Boethius.[316]

The libraries of the Irish monasteries of Würzburg and Reichau seem to have been large and important. Many existing Irish MSS. come from these two monasteries. Unfortunately, no old catalogue of the Würzburg collection seems to have come down to us. In the case of Reichau (Augia Major) on Lake Constance a catalogue was made while Erlebald was abbot between 822 and 838 A.D. The number of MSS. given in this catalogue is 415 of which 30 were written in Erlebald's time.[317]

Important though the collections of Rébais, Würzburg and Reichau undoubtedly were they are overshadowed by the greater fame of Bobbio. Indeed there is only one library that could compare with Bobbio either for the extent or the value of its MSS., and that was the library of St. Gall or Sangallen in Switzerland. This great monastery was founded by St. Gall (in Irish Cellach), the pupil and companion of St. Columbanus, about the year of 612 A.D. In the ninth century the library of St. Gall possessed 533 volumes, nine of them being palimpsests.[318] This library was famous during the Middle Ages. The Fathers who attended the Council of Constance depended mainly for reference on the valuable MSS. in this library to which they had free access; and, sad to relate, when the Council broke up in 1418 A.D. many of these holy men neglected to return these valuable old theological works in Latin and Greek.[319] This same library came to another loss two years earlier, in 1416, when Poggio, the Florentine scholar, with two learned friends who had been engaged at the Council visited St. Gall. Having a season of leisure they made a search for some missing volumes of Cicero, Livy, and other classical writers. Nor were they disappointed. Among other precious tomes they discovered the well-known *Argonauticon* of Flaccus, copies of eight of Cicero's orations with valuable commentaries by Asconius Pedianus, the works of the Roman architect Vitruvius, also the works of Priscian, of Quintilian, of Lucretius, and of other great scholars.[320]

In many libraries of Europe there are MSS. written, or copied, by Irish monks during the seventh, eighth, and ninth centuries. These MSS. are bound together into Codices which are named either after the principal work included therein, or after the monastery where they were written, or sometimes from the library where they are at present deposited. These Codices contain copies of the classics, treatises on grammar, the Psalms, the

Epistles of St Paul, and other portions of the Scriptures, Lives of the Saints, Hymns, Bede's Ecclesiastical History of England, &c. Scribes when studying these often added glosses and scholia either on the margin or between the lines to explain the Latin and Greek words of the text. Sometimes as in the case of the Psalms and of Priscian's grammatical tract these glosses were copious and show that the scribe had availed himself freely of the work of earlier commentators. These glosses have been a rich mine to students of philology and have been extensively used for linguistic purposes containing as they do many of the most archaic forms of the Irish language. The meaning of these Old Irish words can now be obtained from the Greek and Latin words which were originally explained by the Irish words. Some of these MSS. were written by Irishmen on the Continent, while others were written in Ireland and carried to the Continent by other monks who deposited them in the libraries of their monasteries.

LIST[321] OF LIBRARIES CONTAINING MSS. WITH IRISH GLOSSES THEREON NOT LATER THAN END OF NINTH OR BEGINNING OF TENTH CENTURY:

1. Trinity College Library, Dublin.
2. Library of the Franciscan Monastery, Dublin.
3. Royal Irish Academy, Dublin.
4. British Museum, London.
5. Lambert Library, South London.
6. University Library, Cambridge, England.
7. Corpus Christi College, Cambridge.
8. St. John's College, Cambridge.
9. Bodleian Library, Oxford, England.
10. Bibliothèque Nationale, Paris.
11. Library of Nancy.
12. Library of Cambray.
13. University Library, Leyden.
14. University Library, Würzburg.
15. Hof-und Landesbibliothek, Carlsruhe.
16. Royal Library, Munich.
17. Library of the Monastery of Engelberg.

18. Library of St. Paul's Kloster in Carinthia.

19. Royal Library, Dresden.

20. Stadtbibliothek, Schaffhausen.

21. Royal Library, Vienna.

22. Stifsbibliothek, St. Gall.

23. Stadtbibliothek, Berne.

24. Ambrosian Library, Milan.

25. Vatican Library, Rome.

26. University Library, Turin.

27. Biblioteca Nazionale, Turin.

28. Laurentian Library, Florence.

These numerous and valuable MSS. that have come down to us are in themselves the most convincing evidence of the zeal of the Irish monks for the promotion and transmission of classical learning. There can be little doubt that these Irish scholars under the most adverse circumstances fostered learning during the dark ages that preceded the Renaissance and, as we have seen, when the great awakening came one of the sources from which the treasures of classical antiquity emerged were the monastic libraries that contained the MSS. copied, or preserved, with loving care by Irish scribes and scholars.

In this chapter we have endeavoured to show how the zeal for learning which inspired the teacher in the class-room was carried into the scriptorium; how the scribes with patient industry copied, and so transmitted, the relics of classical antiquity; and how these relics were preserved to the afterworld in the great monastic libraries. The direct contribution made by the Irish monks of the Early Middle Ages to contemporary education will be studied in the next chapter. Here we would emphasise the fact that the full significance of the Irish monastic schools as an educational factor cannot be understood unless we realize the importance of the combined, as well as the separate, contribution of these three great centres of intellectual activity, the school, the scriptorium and the library.

CHAPTER VI
COURSE OF STUDIES

Perhaps the question of greatest interest to the student of the history of Education of the Early Middle Ages is the character of curriculum taught in the Irish Monastic Schools during the period under investigation. Most writers have conveniently avoided all reference to this question or they have contented themselves with vague generalizations which may mean much or little in proportion to the reader's own familiarity with the history of the period. We are told, for example, that the Irish monks were possessors of a higher culture than was found elsewhere in Europe and that they taught all the knowledge of their time. Such statements are not particularly helpful. Dr. Joyce, however, has tried to be more explicit. Utilising the materials brought to light through the publication of the Brehon Laws and availing himself of the researches of O'Curry and other Irish scholars, he has compiled[322] two Tables of Degrees and Subjects of Study. In the first he gives the courses of study for Monastic and Bardic Schools in parallel columns. This course appears to have been carefully graded and extends over a period of twelve years. The second table is quite different from the first. It is designated the "Seven Grades or Orders of Wisdom." The former scheme would seem to have the students in view while the latter has reference mainly to the professors or teachers of whom three of the lower grades, or orders, were themselves learners. This shows that in the Irish schools the functions of teaching and learning were closely related, and it often happened that the same person was at one time under instruction of the professors in the grades above him while at another time he was employed in teaching junior scholars.

From an examination of these two schemes we feel justified in drawing the following conclusions:

1. That the scheme of education was carefully graduated and extended over a period of several years, probably from 7 to 26 years in the case of monastic students and from 7 to 30 years for lay students.

2. The lay or bardic studies were limited originally to native secular learning.

3. That the monastic course included both secular and religious studies, that both Latin and the vernacular were used as a medium of instruction, and that the study of native literature was not neglected.

4. That in the monastic school special attention was given to the study of the Sacred Scriptures—both the Old and the New Testament.

5. That there would appear to have been more rote memory work in the Bardic than in the Monastic school.

6. That there was frequent questioning and explanation in the Monastic school.

7. That the degree of Ollamh or Doctor was reserved for those whose learning was profound. That this great scholar was entitled to the highest honour: when he visited the palace he had the privilege of sitting in the banqueting-house with the king.

While we believe the above conclusions fully warranted, we confess that many of the terms used in both schemes are either so vague or so obscure that we do not feel satisfied that an adequate idea of the course of study in the Irish monastic schools can be derived from this source. We propose to supplement Dr. Joyce's helpful but rather meagre account by many additional facts which have been gleaned from an examination of the acknowledged works of Irish writers of this period and such references as are met with in the works of other writers.

We hope to show that the curriculum was a comparatively broad one, including not only the study of the Sacred Scriptures with the commentaries of the Greek and Latin Fathers, but also the study of the pagan authors of Greece and Rome. Nor was the study of the Irish language and literature neglected. Science in the modern sense of the word was unknown, but as regards Geography, Computation, and Astronomy the Irish Monastic Schools were quite as far advanced as any in Europe and certainly far ahead of their neighbours. At least in the ninth century philosophy and dialectic were eagerly studied. We shall have a word to say about the Irish school of church music. Art too flourished, especially the illumination of manuscripts, various ornamental forms of metal work and stone-carving.

No doubt the primary aim of the Irish monastic school was the teaching and study of Christian theology, but just as Christianity itself did not mean the abolition but rather the fulfilment of Hebrew ideals and traditions, so when Christianity was introduced into Ireland where an ancient native culture was flourishing the new culture did not displace the old but rather combined with it to form a new type of culture which in course of time became at once both Irish and Christian. In the schools everything that was not absolutely opposed to the ideals of Christianity was utilised to enrich the course of study. Thus the native laws, literature, music and art became the handmaid of Christianity. The same liberal and enlightened conception of education would explain the success with which the Irish monks pursued the study of the pagan classics. The literary taste already acquired through a study of native literature was entirely favourable to the appreciation and enjoyment of the great authors of antiquity. Besides the Christianity of the Irish monk was sufficiently robust to prevent any of those scruples of conscience which were said to have haunted the continental monk who loved his Virgil.[323] Indeed the stories in the classics about gods and goddesses would be regarded by the Irish purely from a literary and artistic standpoint and could have little religious significance for them since there was little in common between the paganism of Greece and Rome and such remnants of paganism as still survived in Ireland. On the Continent the case was different, hence the suspicion with which continental ecclesiastics regarded the study of writings other than those of the Fathers and as they were ignorant of Greek they had to confine themselves solely to the Latin Fathers. Not so the Irish monks as we shall see later. Moreover, the anxiety to obtain more perfect copies of the Scriptures was an additional and perhaps more powerful incentive to the Irish monk to make himself familiar with the classical forms of Greek and Latin.

If this is a correct interpretation of the educational situation confronting the Irish monastic schools—and the evidence we shall produce is overwhelming—then we shall see how unwarranted is the statement of a recent writer[324] that the learning of the Irish was wholly psalm-singing and theology—not the classics; and that the *maiora studia* referred to by Bede meant the Scriptures,—not philosophy and literature.

STUDY OF THE SCRIPTURES:

We admit that the Scriptures were the great, but by no means the only, subject of study.[325] As early as the fifth century the Irish poet Sedulius wrote his *Carmen Pascale* in which he recounts the chief events of the Old and New Testament giving us "the first Christian epic worthy of the name."[326] The Psalms were learned by rote.[327] The *Book of Armagh* written by an Irish scribe and finished in 807 A.D. contains the only complete copy of the New Testament which has come down from the days of the Celtic Church.[328] The Old Testament lient must have been well known judging from the many existing fragments with glosses and scholia thereon in the handwriting of Irish scribes,[329] not to speak of commentaries like that of Aileran The Wise (d. 665 A.D.)[330] and innumerable Scriptural references in the religious literature of Ireland which is written both in the Gaelic and Latin languages. Indeed so famous were the Irish monastic schools for Scriptural studies that one of the causes which drew foreigners to the Irish schools was the prospect of reading the Sacred Writings in the MSS. so abundantly furnished through the untiring industry of the Irish scribes. Among the more noteworthy visitors who came for this purpose was Agilbert, a native of Gaul, who came in 650 A.D. to Ireland where "he sojourned some time and read the Scriptures."[331] On his return he became bishop of the West Saxons, and later occupied the episcopal see of Paris.[332] The Angle Egbert also spent some time in Ireland "as an exile for Christ that he might study the Scriptures."[333]

The religious education of the Irish monastery was not confined to the singing of hymns and the recitation of psalms as has been asserted. Indeed such exercises formed but a minor part in the monastic scheme. The monks had advanced beyond this elementary stage long before they came to the larger schools.[334] The sacred reading consisted in the study and interpretation of the Bible.[335] Their aim was to search for the spiritual sense and message of the great Book. The higher criticism of these days was then unknown. The investigation of the question of more or less enlightening dates, the details regarding natural life and environment, as well as questions of authorship, the history of particular books, as also all discussion of linguistic and literary form were matters that were wisely left to later times. In the *Interpretatio mystica progenitorum Christi* [336] of Aileran we have an interesting example of a style of commentary which must have been usual in the Irish schools of the seventh century. Aileran quotes not only St. Jerome and St. Augustine but what is more remarkable he cites Origen, the great genius of the Alexandrine school as well as Philo, the Alexandrine Jew.[337] Aileran was not the only Irish monk of the seventh century who showed ability and diligence in research. We have a still more striking example in the case of Cummian Fada (d. 661). Cummian flourished during the years of the Paschal controversy. About the year 630 A.D. a National Synod was held to discuss the advisability of adopting the Roman method of calculating Easter. There was a sharp difference of opinion and owing to insufficiency of information it was necessary to suspend judgment. Cummian was requested to investigate the matter. He tells us how he retired for a whole year into the sanctuary of sacred study to examine as best he could the testimonies of the Scriptures, the facts of history, and the nature of the various cycles in use. The results of his year's study he sums up in his Epistle.[338] He quotes St. Augustine, St. Jerome, St. Cyprian and St. Gregory on the unity of the Church. He then refers to the cycles of Anatolius, Theophilus, Dionysius, Cyril, Morinus, Augustine, Victorius, and Pachomius.[339] In other words his researches showed a wonderful familiarity with the whole subject. In other fields, too, an astonishing range of reading is noticeable; for example, Aengus in his Felire[340] written about 800 A.D. cites Jerome, Ambrose and Eusebius as well as "the countless hosts of the illuminated books of Erin." These examples would at least go to show that the Irish monks had an intimate acquaintance with the writings of the Latin and Greek Fathers but it still remains to be shown that the pagan classical authors were studied.

STUDY OF THE LATIN CLASSICAL AUTHORS:

We have three sources of evidence that the writings of the great classical writers were not neglected as has sometimes been asserted. These sources are: 1, the numerous works of classical authors which have been copied and preserved in the Irish monastic libraries especially those of St. Gall in Switzerland and Bobbio in Italy; 2, the marginal and interlinear glosses on various MSS. earlier than the tenth century; 3, the quotations and imitations of classical writers which are revealed by study of the actual writing of early Irish mediæval writers.

In the section of Chapter V dealing with Irish libraries we discussed fully the first source of evidence and pointed out the influence of these libraries in late mediæval times. In more than one instance we had occasion to refer to the glosses as exemplifying different phases of intellectual activity in the Irish monastic school. Here we would emphasise the fact that these glosses furnish another objective proof that the Irish monks studied and taught the classics as well as the writings of the Fathers. There is considerable variety in the glosses. Generally they are in the nature of explanations written usually in Irish or Latin but occasionally in Greek. They consist mainly of explanations of obscure passages. They give various historical, mythological, and archæological details. They contain definitions, translations of individual words, free translations of idiomatic expressions, illustrations of the correct use of certain words, a summary of the observations of previous commentators and an elucidation of obscure allusions. In short they contain all that varied and supplementary matter which is essential when making an intensive study of a difficult book. These notes were at once grammatical and encyclopædic.[341]

A good example of this kind of work occurs in the *Codex Sangallensis* containing one of the many copies of Priscian's Grammar which were written by Irish scribes. Traube has shown that it was written by some of the friends of Sedulius (of Liège) and supposes that it was copied in some Irish monastery and brought by wandering Irishmen to the Continent. The text is in different hands. The glosses too are in different hands from those which wrote the Latin text. At least three different hands are distinguished.

The authorities relied upon by the glossators are: Origen, Isidore, Jerome, Augustine, Gregory, Hilary, Primascius, Virgilius, Ambrosius, Boethius, Cassianus, Dionysius, Thrax, Gaudentius, Baeda, Orascius, Cicero (not the orator, but an obscure grammarian), Hieronymus, Lactantius, Maximianus, Papirinus, Polibius, Medicus, and Probus.[342]

The very fact of being familiar with such an array of grammarians and authors is enough to justify Sedulius (at Liège 840–860 A.D.) in describing himself and his fellow-countrymen as *docti grammatici*.[343] One of them wrote a treatise on the Art of Versification, *Tractus de Metrica Ratione*,[344] which Zimmer styles a grammatical treatise of importance.[345] Clement (d. 826 A.D.) who succeeded Alcuin as Instructor to the Imperial Court of Charles the Great,[346] *magister palatinus* as he was called, wrote a grammatical work[347] which is famous for its erudition and for the wide range of reading which it shows, especially interesting is his reference to the Greeks "who are our masters in all branches of learning."[348]

These grammatical treatises were much more than books on formal grammar. They dealt with the principles of rhetoric and the art of versification and when enriched by commentaries they must have occupied a prominent place in the educational literature of their own as well as of the succeeding centuries; for we should remember that in those days scholars were inclined to supplement existing works by adding commentaries rather than to attempt anything along original lines. However, many of the Irish monks were accomplished scholars and authors as well as commentators. In this connection many names might be cited, one of the most versatile being Sedulius who taught at Liège from 840 to 860 A.D.[349] Besides writing commentaries on the Scriptures, a grammatical treatise, and a work on the theory of government, he composed numerous poems of much merit.[350] With Sedulius we might rank Donatus (824–874 A.D.), bishop of Fiesole, who was also a poet. Among his poems there is one in which he gives a beautiful description of Ireland and shows that he has a high ideal of the mission of his race. He describes himself as *Scottorum sangine creatus* and tells how he united the duties of bishop to those of teacher of grammar and poetry.[351]

Such varied activities as copying and glossing the writings of classical authors, teaching poetry, and writing treatises on grammar are sufficient to suggest that the literary interests of the Irish monks extended beyond psalm-singing and a study of the writings of the Fathers. Even if their primary interest was the study of the Scriptures this very interest created a need for an abundance of correct texts. This naturally led to a careful study of orthography and the production of treatises on grammar in the broad sense in which we have defined the term. Possibly at first the rudiments of grammar were all that was necessary, but as Mr. Roger so aptly remarks,[352] "l'émulation créée par l'expansion du monachisme, la hardiesse et la curiosité naturelles des Irlandais, le désir d'approcher de plus en plus la pensée divine en pénétrant le sens d'Écriture, le goût pour l'étude qui n'était pas une nouveauté en Irlande, les entraînent au delà de ces éléments." Thus having surmounted preliminary difficulties it was but natural that they whose literary taste had been developed by the study of their vernacular literature should not hesitate to study the classical authors. There was no fear of the return of paganism; to the Irish the Greek and Latin deities made no appeal. As they were not likely to sacrifice their faith to pagan rhetoric there was no necessity to confine themselves to rustic Latin as was the custom with the early Christians on the Continent who were daily drawing farther and farther away from correct classical forms. Hence *a priori* there are many reasons why we should expect to find traces of the classics in the writings of the Irish monks. This view is confirmed by an actual analysis of the existing works of writers of this period.

In the case of the prose works which we have mentioned the more or less technical nature of the subject did not afford scope for the cultivation of a classical style. What was essential was a lucid exposition of the thought-content expressed in clear, correct, intelligible language and this they undoubtedly possessed.[353]

With poetry, however, the case was different. Here naturally enough we find clear traces of the influence of the classical poets, and even in the prose of Irish scholars this same influence is often noticeable. Virgil in particular would appear to have been a special favourite. In this connection it is significant to find Old Irish seventh century glosses on the scholia of Iunius Philargyrius on the Bucolics.[354] Adamnan (624–704 A.D.) knew Virgil well. In his *Vita Sancti Columbae*, as Reeves has pointed out, there is clear evidence that he was familiar with the Georgics.[355] Roger has found traces of both the Georgics and the Aeneid as well as allusions to the authors Plautus and Suetonius.[356] Indeed it has been rigorously established that the extracts from Philargyrius already referred to are the work of no other than Adamnan himself.[357]

Muirchu who wrote the *Memoirs of St. Patrick*, in obedience to the command of Bishop Aed of Sletty (d. 698 A.D.) was inspired by Virgil and perhaps by Apollonius of Rhodes.[358] Columbanus (540–615 A.D.) was in many ways the most striking figure of his time. We have referred to the success of his missionary work.[359] As a classical scholar he was no less remarkable. He did not arrive on the Continent until he was fifty[360] years old and as his life there was filled with missionary work his scholarship must be considered as representative of the Bangor school where he spent so many years of his life as a student and a teacher. Columbanus arrived in Gaul about twenty years before the death of Gregory of Tours. But, as a distinguished French author remarks, it is sufficient to glance at the writings of Columbanus to recognise immediately their marvellous superiority over those of Gregory, or of the Gallo-Romans of his time.[361] He wrote an ode in Adonic verse which abounds in apt classical allusions. [362] In his poetry he imitated or cited Horace and Virgil and he has at least one quotation from the satires of Juvenal. Gundlach who submitted both the prose writings and the poetical Epistolae of Columbanus to a careful investigation, discovered in them quotations from, or reminiscences of, Persius, Virgil, Horace, Sallust, Ovid, Juvenal, as well as of the Christian poets Juvencus, Prudentius and Ausonius.[363] The familiarity with the writings of the classical authors so noticeable in the case of Columbanus is by no means an isolated phenomenon. A period spent in a continental library in exploring the collection of mediæval MSS. seldom fails to be rewarded by the discovery of additional writings of Irish scholars.[364] Thus in recent years Traube found in a MS. in Florence verses[365] composed by an abbot named Cellanus who has been identified with Cellach or Cellanus, the abbot of Peronne who succeeded Ultan, the brother of St. Fursey. Cellanus (d. 706 A.D.) is supposed to be the anonymous monk who wrote a letter to Aldhelm in which the educational influence of Irish scholars in England is referred to.[366] Cellanus, like his contemporary Adamnan, is familiar with Virgil;[367] while Cadoc, a student of Lismore, is said to have known Virgil by rote.[368]

We might give many more instances showing the continuity of Irish classical scholarship during the sixth, seventh and eighth centuries, but enough have been given to appreciate the tribute of Kerr when he says:[369] "The Latin education in Ireland began earlier and was better maintained than in other countries. The English and Teutonic nations received instruction from the Irish, and that not only at the beginning of their studies: Irish learning did not exhaust itself in missionary work and was not merged in the progress of its German pupils; it kept its vivifying power through many generations, and repeated in the ninth century the good works of the fifth, again contributing fresh material and a still rarer spirit of inquiry to the common erudition of the Continent."

That the classical learning carried back into Gaul by the Irish monks did not immediately produce any very encouraging results can be largely accounted for by the disturbed social conditions. The rivalries and weakness of the Merovingian kings prolonged the period of disorder and violence.

Besides, according to Jonas,[370] the negligence of the bishops consequent on the troubled situation was as culpable as the frequency of wars for the decay of religion. Hence the activities of the Irish monks were naturally directed partly at least into other channels in trying to bring about a reform in the morals of the people. To quote Roger:[371] "Tandis que saint Benoît trace, avec sérénité, un plan complet de la vie monastique, saint Columban oppose a la violence des vices, dans une société corrompue, la violence dans la penitence; il trace un plan d'attaque où il met toute la fouge de son caractère. La vertu de la religion était presque abolie; il s'efforce de la ranimer et de rendre à la foi l'efficacité qu'elle avait perdue."

Under the enlightened policy of Charlemagne there was a distinct improvement in the social condition of the people, but the part played by the Irish monks during the seventh and eighth centuries in helping to bring about the moral regeneration of the people must not be overlooked; for even though this aspect of their work lies outside our present study, we cannot completely ignore those social factors which delayed the realization of a literary renaissance until the ninth century. Whether or not the efforts of Charlemagne "resulted in a revival of learning far more important in its consequences than that which is known as *the* Renaissance"[372] it can no longer be questioned that "during the reign of Charlemagne and his immediate successors the chief share of the literary revival which belongs to that period and is known as the Carolingian Renaissance fell to the Irish teachers in Frankland, and if we except Alcuin, Rhabanus and Fredegis, the men who founded that educational system to which the latter Middle Ages owe everything and the modern world more than it generally acknowledges were Irishmen."[373]

STUDY OF GREEK IN EARLY MEDIÆVAL IRELAND:

Having shown that there was an unbroken tradition of classical Latin learning in early mediæval Ireland, having examined the scope and character of that learning and noted its influence in the history of European education, we may fittingly examine the position which Greek occupied in the curriculum of Irish monastic schools. The traditional belief that the study of Greek was pursued in these schools cannot be accepted without investigation in view of the doubts raised by such scholars as Manitius, Roger, and Esposito in recent years.[374] The most important objection raised by these writers is that the evidence is insufficient to justify the claim that the Irish schools possessed a knowledge of Greek prior to the ninth century. Even in the ninth century Esposito will allow the Irish schools no credit for Greek scholarship. According to this writer men like Johannes Scottus Eriugena learned Greek from the books which they found on the

Continent, especially in Gaul. We might retort that these assertions require more proof than has been advanced on their behalf, that these conclusions derive no support from the authorities adduced by Esposito as evidence, and that the views expressed by him are contradicted by the contemporary evidence contained in the well-known passage from Eric the Auxerre.[375]

We believe, however, that the knowledge of Greek for which the Irish schools have been given credit can be established to the satisfaction of the unbiased, just as we have demonstrated the fact that classical Latin was cultivated. In attempting to prove that Greek studies were pursued we are confronted with a difficulty which we did not encounter in our investigation of the question of classical Latin. An examination of the actual writings of Irish scholars who flourished during the sixth, seventh and eighth centuries revealed numerous quotations from, and reminiscences of classical Latin authors, thus we had incontestable evidence of an intimate acquaintance with classical Latin. In studying Greek the aim was not, as in case of Latin, to acquire a new medium of expression, consequently its study would be conducted on different lines. The necessity for such a knowledge existed nevertheless. The great object of study being the Scriptures,[376] the aim of the whole course of study was to prepare men's minds for the "Lectio Divina," their one great science to which all the other "disciplinae" were but auxiliaries. It is therefore but reasonable to suppose that the Irish monks were impelled towards a study of Greek, a knowledge of which was so necessary in studying the Scriptures. This view is corroborated by an examination of native Irish sources. Thus Dallan Forgal in his eulogy of Colmcille (composed c. 576 A.D.) says: "Atgaill grammataig greic," that is, "he taught Greek Grammar."[377] The early glossaries swarm with Greek words quoted for etymological purposes.[378] The hymns in the *Antiphonary* of Bangor contain numerous Greek words.[379] Indeed, the charms of the Greek language had such a fascination for Irish writers that many of them had developed a pedantic turn as early as the seventh century.[380] Zimmer has pointed out the Greek of these early writers was not merely bookish learning but a living speech.[381] Meyer's tabulation of the peculiarities in the transcription of Greek as practised by Irish writers confirms the accuracy of Zimmer's observation.[382] We are informed that a Greek taught Mosinu MacCuimin "the art of computation."[383] Keller gives numerous examples of Hiberno-Greek characters.[384] In an eighth century MS. of Adamnan's *Vita Sancti Columbae* there are many instances which suggest that the Greek and Roman characters, as written by the Irish scribes, mutually affected each other and gave the Irish alphabet especially in the capitals that peculiar character which distinguishes it from all others. [385] In the *Book of Armagh* written about 807 A.D. there are several Greek words and the Lord's Prayer is written in Greek characters.[386] In the glosses on Priscian's Grammar Greek words and phrases are explained by Irish equivalents and we note a familiarity with the rules of Greek grammar. [387] The most remarkable evidence is that of Aldhelm[388] who in a letter to Eahfrid fresh from the Irish schools finds fault with him for having gone to the "didasculi Argivi" of that country instead of staying in England where Theodore of Tarsus and Hadrian of Nisida[389] had introduced Greek studies. It is significant that this letter of Aldhelm's abounds in Hellenisms to a greater extent than any of his other writings, his object being apparently to impress Eahfrid with the Greek learning to be obtained in England.

We have referred to a common practice of the Irish monks, viz., the making of marginal and interlinear glosses in which were explained Latin, Greek and even sometimes Hebrew words and expressions by Irish equivalents. They also compiled lists of Irish words which were considered difficult or obsolete at the time the glosses were written. These words were explained by giving their more modern equivalents. Frequently the meaning was given in Latin and Greek also. The most famous glosses of this class are Cormac's[390] and O'Mulconry's glosses.[391] Dr. Hyde describes[392] Cormac's glossary "as by far the oldest attempt[393] at a comparative vernacular dictionary made in any language of modern Europe. The king-bishop (Cormac, d. 903 A.D.) was a most remarkable man and an excellent scholar. He appears to have known Latin, Greek, Hebrew and Danish and to have been one of the finest old Gaelic scholars of his day and withal an accomplished poet." In the library of St. Paul in Lavanthale (Steyermark) there is a MS. full of extracts written by an Irish monk. It contains Irish poems of the eighth century, Latin hymns, the commencement of a commentary on Virgil, a treatise on astronomy, *Greek declensions and paradigms as well as a Greek vocabulary.*[394] The Greek Creed was sung in the churches of St. Gallen.[395] Under the title *Proverbia Graecorum* there is a collection of sayings translated by some Irish scholar from Greek into Latin before the seventh century.[396] In the eighth century Boniface brings Clement the Irishman to task for not accepting the teaching of the Latin Fathers Jerome, Augustine and Gregory, just as a century later Scottus Eriugena was charged with being inclined too much to the Greek Fathers and with under-rating the Latin Fathers.[397] In the library of Laon there is a MS. written by an Irish scribe between the years 850–900 A.D. This MS. contains two glossaries in the Greek and Latin languages with occasional passages in the Irish language. It also contains a Greek grammar.[398] It is believed that the *Hermeneumata* of the Pseudo-Dositheus, a text used by Roman boys in studying Greek, as well as the work of Macrobius were only saved for the afterworld because they were used by the Irish.[399] The interlinear Latin versions of Greek texts are of exclusively Irish origin.[400] In the department of Biblical study Zimmer recalls two important examples: the Gospel Codex of St. Gallen written in Greek with a Latin translation and the Codex Boernerianus, now in Dresden, which contains the Epistles of St. Paul in Greek together with an interlinear Latin version. Both belong to the ninth century.[401]

These various examples of a knowledge of Greek and of the necessary materials for teaching it, such as grammars, paradigms, vocabularies and glosses, as well as interlinear translations clearly point to the conclusion that Greek was taught in the Irish monastic schools of the seventh and eighth centuries. In our next chapter when we come to examine the scope of Irish scholarship, the knowledge of Greek will be so evident in the case of the great ninth century scholars like Sedulius of Liège, Dungal of Pavia, Clement the successor of Alcuin at the Palace School and Scottus Eriugena that it is unnecessary to discuss the matter further at present. The question as to where these scholars got their classical training can be answered best by saying that they got it in the monastic schools of Ireland where we have shown that the classical tradition was unbroken from at least as early as the sixth century, possibly a century or two earlier.[402]

De Jubainville declares that in the ninth century the Irish scholars were the only persons in Western Europe who knew Greek.[403] Traube claims that in the time of Charles the Bald at least the Irish were the sole representatives of Greek scholarship: "they could read and write Greek, they could transcribe it, nay, they even ventured occasionally to make Greek verses."[404] Anyone who in the time of Charles the Bald was credited with a knowledge of Greek was, according to Traube, an Irishman, or had learned it from an Irishman, or his reputation for Greek scholarship was a fraud. [405] It is significant that the copy of the work of Dionysius the Areopagite, which Pope Paul had presented to King Pippin had to wait for an Irishman, Johannes Scottus Eriugena, to translate it for Charles the Bald.[406]

That a knowledge of Greek was indispensable for a study of the Scriptures would in itself be sufficient to account for the study of Greek in the Irish monastic schools. A further reason for the Irish love of Greek has been suggested by several writers. Michelet says: "Le génie celtique, qui est celui de l'individualité, sympathise profondément avec le génie grec."[407] As we have pointed out, the Greek views in philosophy and theology appealed in an especial manner to Irish scholars of this period. According to Healy, "the Irish mind, like the Greek, has a natural love for speculation, is quick, subtle, and far-seeing, has greater power of abstraction and generalization — that is, greater metaphysical power than the phlegmatic Anglo-Saxon."[408] We venture no opinion as to whether this proposition will stand a critical examination but would merely record the fact that other able writers when dealing with this period have also discerned much in common between the Hellenic and the Celtic mind. Mullinger notes "a certain speculative, outlooking quality certainly not very apparent in the school of York."[409] Cardinal Newman declares that as Rome was the centre of authority in these ages so Ireland was the native home of speculation; while contrasting the English scholars with the Irish he says: "The Englishman was hardworking, plodding, bold, determined, persevering, obedient to law and precedent, and if he cultivated his mind he was literary rather than scientific. In Ireland, on the other hand, the intellect seems to have taken the line of science and we have various instances to show how fully this was recognised. 'Philosopher' in these times is almost synonymous with 'Irish Monk'."[410] It was this characteristic of the Irish monks Renan[411] had in mind when he spoke of them as "les colonisateurs scientifiques d'Europe occidentale."

A further resemblance, and one of a less promising character, may be traced in the predilection shown by both the Greek and the Gael for questions which admitted a display of dialectical subtlety. It was this feature which arrested the attention of Benedict of Aniane and aroused his dislike for the Irish theologians. They were distinguished, he tells us, for syllogistic mystification. "Apud modernos scholasticos maxime apud Scottos iste syllogismus delusionis."[412] Mullinger tells us that they would sometimes amuse themselves by interrogating some stolid representative of orthodoxy, and compel him as a logical sequence of his replies, to admit the existence of three Gods or to disavow his belief in the Trinity.[413] This typically national characteristic of adding a humorous touch to a profound but dry metaphysical discussion has for us a deep human interest, though it was undoubtedly embarrassing to learned and solemn opponents who could neither understand, nor sympathise with, the rather subtle and complex Irish temperament.

It has also been remarked that this tendency to speculation led the Irish to admire the work of Martianus Capella whose volume was a sealed book to the school of York; while in the three great monasteries of Luxeuil, St. Gall, and Bobbio numerous MSS. in the original Irish character (Scottice scripta) of Origen and other Greek Fathers remained to attest the more inquiring spirit in which the studies of their communities were pursued. Thanks to his Greek studies and his natural mental attitude the Irish Theologian became a better astronomer as well as a better dialectician.[414]

MUSIC:

Music constituted an important element in Irish culture both in pagan and in Christian times. Hectateus, the great geographer quoted by Diodorus, is the first who mentions the name Celt and he describes the Celts of Ireland as singing songs in praise of Apollo and playing melodiously on the harp (c. 500 B.C.).[415] Native Irish literature abounds in reference to music and musicians who were always spoken of in terms of the highest respect. Everywhere through these ancient records we find evidence that the Irish people both high and low were passionately fond of music. It entered into their daily lives and formed a part of their amusements and celebrations of every kind.[416] Zeuss in his *Grammatica Celtica* (1853) was the first to give the key to the nature of the musical instruments used in ancient Ireland. The references to music given by Zeuss were taken from glosses dating from 650 A.D. to 900 A.D. and written by the Irish monks of St. Gall. O'Curry,[417] Joyce,[418] and Flood[419] have followed up the work of Zeuss, so we have now a fairly clear idea of the state of musical culture during the period under investigation. Flood gives the names of twelve different instruments in use and of nine professional names of the performers.[420] It is not without significance that the harp is the national symbol. There are references to the harp in Irish literature probably as early as the fifth century.[421] O'Curry was so impressed with the many evidences he found of a high degree of musical culture that he could not restrain his enthusiasm. He says: "If ever there was a people gifted with a musical soul and sensibility in a higher degree than another I would venture to assert that the Ancient Gaedhil of Ireland were that people."[422]

The monks were no exception to their fellow-countrymen in their love of music, consequently in Christian times music was intimately connected with public worship.[423] In the early ages of the Church many of the Irish ecclesiastics took delight in playing the harp and in order to indulge this innocent and refining taste they were wont to take with them a small portable harp when going from place to place.[424] Figures of men playing the harp are common on the stone crosses seen at Graig, Ullard, Clonmacnoise, Durrow and Monasterboice, as also on the shrines of ancient reliquaries. [425] It appears from several authorities that the practice of playing on the harp as an accompaniment to the voice was common in Ireland as early as the fifth or sixth century.[426]

During the long period when learning flourished Irish professors and teachers of music would seem to have been quite as much in request as teachers of literature and philosophy. In the middle of the seventh century Gertrude (daughter of Pepin, Mayor of the Palace) when abbess of Niville in Belgium engaged Foillan and Ultan brothers of St. Fursey to instruct her nuns in Psalmody.[427] It has been asserted that Gregorian chant coloured much of the music of Ireland from the fifth to the eighth century, but Gregorian chant dates only from 593 A.D. and, as Flood pointed out, both the psalmody and the hymnody of the Irish were distinctly Celtic in the first half of the seventh century and were mainly adaptations of the old pre-Christian melodies.[428]

The musical fame of St. Gall monastery in Switzerland is known to many, but the fact is often ignored that its foundation in 612 A.D. is due to the Irish saint Cellach whose name has been latinised Gallus or Gall. St. Gall was a student of the monastery of Bangor (in Co. Down, Ireland) and the friend and pupil of Columban whom he accompanied to the Continent. When St. Gall died in 645 A.D. the fame of his music school had spread far and near.[429] In the year 870 A.D. Moengal, another Irishman, was appointed headmaster of the Music School of St. Gall and under his rule it became "the wonder and delight of Europe."[430] Moengal laboured for ten years on behalf of the school. It should be added that Moengal was also learned in theology and secular sciences. "Erat in divinas et humanis eruditissimus."[431] The copying of music became such a feature of the work done at St. Gall that "the scribes of this monastery supplied all Germany with manuscript books of the Gregorian Chant, all beautifully illuminated."[432] Moengal gave music its highest place amongst the arts and the school of St. Gall reached its highest perfection under three of Moengal's pupils, Ratpert, Notker and Tuotilo.[433] In Zimmer's opinions there were very few men who exercised such a beneficent influence over Germany in the ninth century as did Moengal and his successors.[434]

Moengal was succeeded in 890 A.D. by Tuathal (latinised Tuotilo and sometimes Tutilo), his pupil and fellow-countryman. Tuotilo (d. 915 A.D.) was even more famous than his master and was not only a skilled musician but was famed as a poet, orator, painter, goldsmith, builder and sculptor. We are told that he was a skilled performer on the cruit and psaltery. Père Schubiger published many of the *tropes* composed by Tuotilo. Flood assures us that two of these *Hodie Cantandus* and *Omnipotens Genator* betray the well-known characteristics of Irish music.[435] Tuotilo also composed the famous farced *Kyrie, Fons Bonitatis*, included in the Vatican collection of Kyriale.[436]

Another famous pupil of Moengal's was Notker or Notker Balbulus the author of a valuable collection of hymns known as *Liber Ymnorum Notkeri* which was illuminated by an Irish artist. Notker shed undying lustre on the school of St. Gall and was one of the most celebrated musicians of the Middle Ages.[437]

St. Gall was not the only monastery of Irish origin in which the study of music was pursued with success. Indeed, the musical influence of the Irish monks was felt over the whole west of Europe wherever their monasteries were established, not only in Ireland and Scotland but also throughout a large part of England, France, Belgium, Germany, Italy and Austria.[438]

Hymnologists are more or less familiar with the hymns composed by Irish poets such as Sedulius, Dungal and Moengal, and by saints like Sechnall, Columba, Molaise, Cuchuimne, Columban, Ultan, Colman, Cummian, Aengus, Fiacc, Brodan, Sanctan and Moelisu.[439]

Thus did the Irish monks both by their teaching and by their writings promote the cultivation of music in a very practical way. Nor was the theoretical aspect of music neglected. Donnchadh, an Irish bishop of the ninth century, who died abbot of Remigius, wrote a commentary on the work of Martianus Capella, a well-known volume on the "Liberal Arts," a section of which treats of music. The greatest of his contemporaries, Johannes Scottus Eriugena, in his famous philosophical work *De Divisione Naturae*, written in 867 A.D. expounds *organum* or *discant* a hundred years before the appearance of *Scholia Enchiriadis* and *Musica Enchiriadis*.[440] He also wrote a commentary on *Martianus Capella* which is now in a Paris MS. of the ninth century.[441]

Summarising the history of Irish music prior to the close of the ninth century Flood says:[442] "The Irish were acquainted with the Ogam music tablature in pre-Christian ages; they had battle marches, dance tunes, folk songs, chants and hymns in the fifth century; they were the earliest to adopt the neums or neumatic notation for the plain chant of the Western Church; they modified and introduced Irish melodies into the Gregorian Chant; they had an intimate acquaintance with the diatonic scale long before it was perfected by Guido of Arezzo. They were the first to employ harmony and counterpoint; they had quite an array of bards and poets; they employed blank verse, elegiac rhymes, consonant, assonant, inverse, burthen, dissyllabic, trisyllabic, and quadrisyllabic rhymes, not to say anything of the caoines, laments, elegies, metrical romances, etc.; they had a world-famed school of harpers, and finally they diffused musical knowledge over Europe."

ART:

A lengthy discussion of the subject of Irish art lies outside the scope of our present study. We shall therefore content ourselves with making a rapid survey of some of its more characteristic features and with noting the part played by the monastic schools in its development and cultivation.

In the first chapter it was pointed out that there was a native art in Ireland before the introduction of Christianity and that the pagan Irish exhibited considerable artistic skill in their bronze, silver, gold, and enamel work as the specimens still preserved in our museums go to prove. From the pagan period we have numerous torques, gorgets, lunulae and other articles of personal adornment. These show that the pagan artist possessed both skill and taste in a high degree.[443] The character of the arts introduced into Ireland with Christianity was therefore grafted upon and modified by the native arts while new variations in design were introduced from the Continent by missionaries and foreign artists that came to Ireland. Thus art as practised in early Christian Ireland was no slavish imitation of foreign art but rather a development of native art whose progress was upward from the introduction of Christianity in the fourth and fifth century until the Norman invasion in the twelfth.[444]

CHARACTERISTICS OF IRISH ART:

The chief characteristics of Irish art are:

1. A symmetrical interlacement of a band or bands into a variety of patterns.

2. The graceful divergence of lines into trumpet forms.

3. The coiling of one or two very fine lines into mysterious spirals a lengthened examination of which has a weirdly fascinating effect on the eye.

4. A total disregard for the comforts of animal life, the bodies and members being twisted and distorted to suit the convenience of the artist.

5. The human figure is frequently introduced, but it is subjected to the rigidity of the curved lines noticeable in the interlacings and spirals. Herein Irish art, which is primarily *ornamental,* differs from classic art, which is *representative.* The Irish artist aimed at symmetry and hence the right side of the face is generally a reproduction of the left.

6. In nearly all the art of the period under consideration the ground is divided into panels, or geometrical compartments—an arrangement whereby the artist whether working on vellum, metal, leather or stone was free to introduce any of the foregoing characteristics without marring the harmony and uniformity of the design.[445]

Irish art attained its highest excellence in four branches, namely, writing and illumination of manuscripts, metal work and stone carving. In a previous chapter were discussed the characteristics of the Irish style of handwriting and the part played by the monastic schools in its development so we pass on to consider the other three departments of art work.

ILLUMINATION:

Shortly after the Irish monks became skilled penmen they began to illuminate their books with brilliant colours which they learned to combine into elaborate and harmonious designs. This art reached its most perfect stage of development at the close of the eighth or beginning of the ninth century. The monks were wont to lavish all the wealth of their artistic skill on books containing the whole or portions of the Holy Scriptures. As instances of this style of illuminated MSS. the *Psalter of ColmCille*, the *Book of Dimma*, the *Book of Armagh*, and, above all, the *Book of Kells* should be mentioned. While each of these books has many merits the book which has compelled the admiration yet defied the imitation of every European artist is the *Book of Kells*. Describing this venerable volume which was written and illuminated about the middle of the ninth century, Sir Edward O'Sullivan writes as follows:[446] "Its weird and commanding beauty; its subdued and goldless colouring; the baffling intricacy of its fearless designs; the clean unwavering sweep of rounded spiral; the creeping undulations of serpentine forms that writhe in artistic profusion throughout the mazes of its decorations; the strong and legible minuscule of the text; the quaintness of its striking portraiture; the unwearied reverence and patient labour which brought it into being, all of which combined to make the *Book of Kells*, have raised this ancient volume to a position of abiding pre-eminence amongst the illuminated MSS. of the world."

Other artists are equally emphatic in their praises of the work of Irish artists during the period under consideration.

Westwood writes: "Ireland may justly be proud of the *Book of Kells*. ... At a period when the fine arts may be said to be almost extinct in Italy and other parts of the Continent, nearly from the fifth to the end of the eighth century, the art of ornamenting MSS. had a perfection almost miraculous in Ireland. ... The invention and skill displayed, the neatness, precision, and delicacy far surpass all that is found in MSS. executed by Continental artists."[447]

Referring to the interlaced style of ornament introduced in the seventh and eighth century Coffey[448] informs us that this new style with all its intricacy was brought to a marvellous perfection in the Irish monastic schools. The same writer further assures us that the Irish MSS. (with which he would class the Hiberno-Saxon MSS. in the production of which the Irish scribes took such important a part) admittedly stand in quite the first place among early MSS. for the excellence of their penmanship and illustrations.

As showing that the Irish style of art had more than a local influence the testimony of another art critic, Mr. Digby Wyatt, is worth quoting. He says:

"In close connection with the Irish church existed a school of art remarkable for its sense of the graceful and grotesque, and for its superiority in point of ornamental design to any other style of the same period. That its influence extended much farther than is generally supposed would appear certain, and not only did Scotland, Wales, Cornwall, the North of England and Scandinavia adopt its peculiar system of ornament, but some of the MSS. in the libraries of Europe are now discovered to have emanated from this school."[449]

The colours of the *Book of Kells* are remarkably well preserved after a lapse of one thousand years. Professor Hartley[450] a few years ago submitted the pigments to a careful examination and discovered the materials of which the colours are most probably compounded. He reported as follows: "The black is lampblack, or possibly fishbone black; the bright red is realgar (arsenic disulphide As2S2) the yellow, orpiment (arsenic tersulphide As2S3); the emerald green, malachite; the deep blue possibly lapis lazuli, but owing to its transparency when overlying green more likely not so. The reddish purple is either finely ground glass obtained from a solution of gold, or a preparation which was obtained by the action of a solution of tin and was very expensive. The other colours are neutral green like burnt sienna, a pale blue, and lilac."[451]

ART METAL WORK:

We have referred to the fact that the pagan Irish were skilled workmen in metal. This class of work received a new impetus with the introduction of Christianity. The pre-Christian craftsmen exercised their skill in ornamenting shields, swords, sword-hilts, chariots, brooches, bridles, etc. as we learn from the specimens that are preserved in our museums.[452] In addition to articles of this class the Christian artists, the majority of whom were ecclesiastics,[453] made crosses, croziers, chalices, shrines to hold books or relics as well as book satchels in which both metal and leather were used. [454] Specimens of these may be seen in the National Museum, Dublin.[455] For real artistic skill the most admired specimens are the Ardagh Chalice, the Tara Brooch, and the Cross of Cong.[456] The designs and styles of ornament used by the metal workers were similar to those of the artists who illuminated the MSS. Artistic skill in metal work was brought to its highest degree of excellence in the tenth and eleventh centuries and continued to flourish until about the end of the twelfth century, but gradually declined after that date owing to the general disorganization of society consequent on the Norman invasion.[457]

STONE CARVING:

The skill of the Irish artists in stone carving is seen at its best in the great stone crosses of which about 55 remain in different parts of Ireland. One peculiarity of the Irish (or Celtic) Cross is the circular ring round the intersections, thus binding the arms together. This peculiar form was developed in Ireland and, once developed, remained fixed from the eighth to the twelfth century. Of the 55 great crosses 35 are richly ornamented and eight have inscriptions bearing names of persons who have been identified as living at various dates from 904 to 1150 A.D.[458]

The crosses have a style of ornamentation similar to that of the manuscripts and of the metal work. In addition to the ornamentation most of the crosses have groups of figures representing various events in Sacred History, such as, The Fall of Man, Noah in the Ark, The Sacrifice of Isaac, The Fight of David and Goliath, The Arrest of Our Lord, The Crucifixion, The Crucifixion of St. Peter (head downward), Eve Presenting the Apple to Adam, The Journey to Egypt. These sculptures are *iconographic, i.e.* they were intended to bring to the minds of the unlettered people the facts of Sacred History by vivid illustration. No doubt the preachers in their discourses directed the attention of their hearers to these representations; and perhaps they often lectured while standing at the foot of the cross with the people ranged in front, the preacher pointing to the sculptured groups as occasion demanded. It is probable that the figures were painted in brilliant colours like those used in illuminating the MSS. so that the people might see them more distinctly.[459]

MATHEMATICS AND SCIENCE:

We cannot close our discussion of the curriculum of Irish monastic schools without a brief reference to its limitations which are especially noteworthy in the case of mathematics and other secular sciences. While not venturing into details some writers manage to convey the impression that the scientific knowledge of the Irish monks was as profound as their knowledge of the classics. We have not found any evidence to support this view. The most that can be said in favour of the teachers of this early period is that they willingly imparted all the mathematical and scientific knowledge of their time. But the actual amount of such knowledge possessed by Western Europe prior to the tenth century was relatively small as compared with even the later Middle Ages not to speak of modern times.

ARITHMETIC:

Prior to the tenth century arithmetic was essentially the art of computation. It was largely devoted to computing Easter, so the terms

"Computus" and "Arithmetic" became synonymous.[460]   Apart from this practical side it is possible that a theoretical treatment of numbers was not absolutely wanting. The method of reckoning was necessarily crude and little progress was possible while the cumbersome Roman system of notation made computation with large numbers well nigh impossible. It remains for further investigation to show whether the arithmetical knowledge of the Irish monks extended beyond the limits of Bede's *De Tempora Ratione*,[461] or equalled that of the *Liber de Computo* [462] of Rabanus Maurus. Our acquaintance with source material in this field is too limited to warrant any sweeping statement, but it is significant of the nature of arithmetical knowledge of this period and of the lack of creative ability to find a scholar of such ability as Marianus Scottus in the following century basing his work on Computus[463] on that of Rabanus. Indeed it was not until the introduction of the Arabic system of notation and Hindoo methods through Arabic influence that there was much possibility of progress in Arithmetic. The introduction of the Arabic system is attributed by some to Gerbert[464] (d. 1003 A.D.) but it was not until the end of the twelfth century that the Hindoo-Arabic system became generally established among mathematicians. A century later Arithmetic began to be applied to commerce.[465]

Algebra was apparently unknown to the Irish monks during the period under investigation and was probably not introduced into Europe until the twelfth century.[466]

GEOMETRY:

Up to the tenth century, the age of Gerbert, a knowledge of Geometry in our sense of the term hardly existed in Western Europe. In fact the term seems to have been used in its etymological meaning and not in the sense the Greeks understood it. We have found no evidence to warrant the assumption that Euclidean Geometry was taught in those early Irish monastic schools. But on the other hand an examination of the characteristic Irish style of ornament suggests that the Irish artist had at least a good working knowledge of practical Geometry. Possibly the amount of knowledge of theoretical Geometry did not extend beyond the narrow[467] limits of the works of Capella,[468] Cassiodorus,[469] and Isadore of Seville[470] — writers well known to Irish scholars as we have seen.

GEOGRAPHY:

If the mathematical science of Geometry was still undeveloped in the West geography, topography and cosmography made up the deficiency. It was but natural that the Irish monks, the greatest voyagers of their time, should be interested in the study of foreign lands. We have an instance of this in the case of Adamnan who wrote his *De Locis Sanctis* from the dictation of Arculfus, a Frankish bishop who had visited Palestine.[471] Bede based his work bearing a similar name on Adamnan's volume. This work of Adamnan with that of Bede continued to be the only source of information of the geography, Christian antiquities, and customs of Palestine until the Crusades gave Western Europe a more acute and active interest in that distant, inhospitable region.[472] We have referred to a curious geographical poem[473] which was evidently used as a text in the monastic schools of Ireland. It contained probably all the geography that was taught prior to the tenth century. The tenth century map of the world[474] drawn in England for an Anglo-Saxon is supposed to have been the work of an Irish artist and further illustrates the state of geographical knowledge of the times. The more ambitious treatise of Dungal, *De Mensura Orbis Terrarum*, which will be described in the next chapter, marks a new departure in geographical texts—hitherto mere compendiums—inasmuch as it introduces new matter, is more critical, "up-to-date" and altogether a commendable attempt for a ninth century scholar.

Astronomy had a double interest for the Irish monks. Being great travellers in an age when they had no compass to direct their way the "study of the stars" was a matter of practical interest and possibly they were more observant of the courses of the heavenly bodies than the majority of us are to-day. Again, the ability to compute the date of Easter was a matter of great importance in ecclesiastical circles in those days. The controversies which centred around the Easter question caused many Irish monks to give special attention to practical methods of computing the date of Easter. They were also led to examine the history of the different cycles in use and finally they were led to inquire into the theoretical aspect of the science of Astronomy. In the present chapter we referred to the famous Paschal Epistle of Cummian Fada which showed that he was at one and the same time an accomplished classical scholar and an astronomer of no mean ability versed in all astronomical literature of his time. Other great astronomers were Virgilius, Dicuil and Dungal, of whom we shall have something to say in our next chapter when dealing with the scope of Irish monastic scholarship. Of all the secular sciences Astronomy was perhaps the most popular with Irish monastic scholars the superiority of whose scholarship in this regard is acknowledged by all writers of the early Middle Ages.[475]

We see, then, that though the actual amount of mathematical and scientific knowledge possessed by the Irish monks was small they freely taught all that was known at the time in Western Europe and, limited as was their educational equipment, we may safely conclude that it represented the maximum attainments in western scientific knowledge prior to the tenth century.

While we have no means of determining the precise way in which the curriculum was organised, we may safely conclude that it embraced the following groups of studies:

1. *Vernacular Studies*: The Irish language, its grammar, metrics, literature both secular and religious, prose and poetry, history, antiquities, etc.[476]

2. *Christian Studies*: Theology, especially the study of the Scriptures with the commentaries of the Fathers thereon, and in the ninth century at least the study of Dialectics and Philosophy was pursued with success.

3. *Classical Studies*: Acquaintance with several Latin and Greek authors of the classical period. Superior knowledge of Latin and a good working knowledge of Greek.

4. *Aesthetic Studies*: Cultivation of Art and Music.

5. *Scientific Studies*: All the scientific knowledge of the time, special emphasis on Computation and Astronomy.

Thus we see that the course of studies of the early Irish monastic school was much more varied in scope and fuller in content than the Trivium and Quadrivium as taught in contemporary Europe.

CHAPTER VII
SCOPE AND INFLUENCE OF
IRISH SCHOLARSHIP

In the preceding chapter we discussed at length the nature of the curriculum of the Irish monastic schools. Our conclusions were based on the evidence supplied by an examination of the writings and other material remains which attest their Irish authorship. Here we shall attempt to determine the extent as well as the limitations of Irish scholarship, and briefly indicate the influence which that scholarship may reasonably claim to have exerted on the history of mediæval education. As illustrations of types of Irish scholars who attained eminence in a special field and yet displayed considerable versatility we have selected five: Virgilius, Dicuil, Dungal, Sedulius and Eriugena. These may fairly be considered as representing Irish scholarship of the period at its best.[477] All except Virgilius belong to the ninth century.

Virgilius, bishop of Salzburg (766–7–784–5 A.D.) whose name is a latinised form of the Irish name Fearghal, was one of the few men who in the eighth century cultivated the profane sciences.[478] Indeed the age in which he lived was equally unfavourable to the pursuit of science or to the encouragement of speculative thought, as Virgilius found from experience. On one occasion, Boniface, the Papal Legate, denounced him for promulgating false doctrines inasmuch as he maintained that the sun and moon passed under the earth, and that there must be inhabitants on the other side.[479] Boniface had a previous dispute with Virgilius over a theological question in which the Pope decided in favour of Virgilius. Either from ignorance of Astronomy or, as some think, through pique, Boniface appears to have misrepresented the real views of Virgilius so as to convey the impression that he taught that there was another world and another sun and moon and consequently other men who were not redeemed by Our Lord.[480] The versions of Virgilius' teaching which we have given would appear to represent his real views on the subject. At any rate he seems to have explained his doctrine to the satisfaction of the Pope; for we find no further mention of the controversy and he retained his see until his death in 784–5 A.D.[481] His teachings show that he must have held that the world was spherical, though he was wrong in his theory that the sun and stars revolved round the earth. Even this semi-correct theory was a decided advance on contemporary views on astronomical matters and shows that Virgilius was an original thinker on scientific subjects, or else it argues for his acquaintance with Greek literature in which he may have become familiar with the doctrine of Eudoxus and Eratosthenes, as to the sphericity of the earth.[482] As Virgilius was bishop of Aghaboe in Ireland before he went to the Continent, it is most improbable that he received his education any place other than in an Irish monastic school. Unlike many of the Irish scholars who went abroad the name of Virgilius is recorded in the Irish annals, a circumstance which would lead us to suppose that he was already famous for his scholarship before he went abroad. An additional reason for believing that he had acquired a reputation as a scientist is the fact that he is called in the annals Virgil or Fergal the "Geometer."[483]

Dicuil (d. 825 A.D.) is another instance of an Irish scholar who was interested in secular studies. His chief claim to fame rests on a Latin tract entitled *De Mensura Orbis Terrarum*.[484] As the name would suggest, this was a work of geography in the sense that the term is now used. The internal evidence leaves no doubt as to the Irish birth and education of the author. He speaks of *nostri Scoti, nostra insula Hibernia*, alludes to the Irish poet Sedulius whom he styles *noster Sedulius* and he shows an accurate knowledge of the islands near Britain and Ireland.[485] He tells that a certain Suibneus (in Irish Suibhne anglicised Sweeney) was his master to whom under God he owed whatever knowledge he possessed. This Suibhne has been identified with Suibhne, abbot of Clonmacnoise, who died 810 A.D.[486] This would suggest that Dicuil was a pupil of the famous school of Clonmacnoise.

He derived his material from three sources:

1. He utilised the report of the Theodosian survey. He tells us that he made it the basis of his work because though vitiated by false MSS. it was less faulty than Pliny especially in its measurements.

2. He utilised the works of previous geographers.

3. He made several interesting additions to existing knowledge which he derived from trustworthy accounts of Irish monks who were the greatest travellers of the time.

The list of authors from whom he borrowed is very large, including Pliny, Solinus, Isidore, Virgil, Crosius, Servius, Hectateus, Homer, Herodotus and other Greek writers.[487]

Dicuil is the first writer to refer to Iceland, which he describes under the name Thule from an account given to him by some Irish monks who visited that island about thirty years previously (c. 795 A.D.) and remained there from February to August.

He was also the first to give authentic information about the Faroe Islands, which were visited by Irish hermits a hundred years before, but were forsaken on account of the piratical incursions of the Northmen.

The truth of these interesting accounts is proved in two ways: 1, the tolerably exact statements as to the length and shortness of the days could only be determined by a resident of the place; 2, from northern and independent sources we learn that the first Norwegian settlers who were of course pagans found Christians whom they called *Papar*. These Papar left Irish books, croziers, bells and other things behind them when they went away.[488]

When describing the Nile he introduces the narrative of a brother Fidelis who with a party of priests and monks made a journey from Ireland to the Holy Land.[489]

To be fair to Dicuil, we must judge his work not by modern scientific standards but by the standards of the ninth century. We must at least acknowledge that he made a genuine effort to obtain the most accurate available information and that he was more than usually conscientious, for when Pliny's figures seemed to him to be inaccurate, he left a blank space. [490]

In addition to the *Liber de Mensura Orbis Terrarum*, Dicuil is the author of a short poem of twenty hexameters which he prefixed to a copy of a short treatise by Priscian,[491] and of an astronomical work in prose and verse which is still unpublished.[492] This latter is dedicated to Louis the Pious and mentions Dicuil by name. We may therefore infer that this geographer, astronomer and poet was one of the versatile Irish scholars whose work must have contributed in no small degree to the Carolingian revival of learning. This distinguished scholar is believed to be identical with the Dicuil who was abbot of Pahlacht in the ninth century.[493]

Dungal is another of those ninth century scholars of whose life the details are all too meagre. From a few fragmentary references and his existing works we are led to the conclusion that he was a very capable man distinguished not only as a theologian and poet but also as an astronomer and schoolmaster.[494]

In the year 811 A.D. he wrote a letter to Charlemagne to explain the double eclipse of the sun that was supposed to have occurred the previous year. This letter is written in excellent Latin showing familiarity with Virgil and Cicero.[495]

Moreover it shows an intimate acquaintance with the whole field of astronomical literature of the time, but it is chiefly remarkable for the expression of astronomical views that were considered advanced because they seemed to call in question the truth of the Ptolemaic system.[496]

In the year 825 A.D. the Emperor Lothair desiring to carry out the enlightened educational policy of his ancestor Charlemagne issued an Edict[497] complaining that through the extreme carelessness and indolence of certain superiors true teaching was shaken to its very foundations, and urging that persons engaged in teaching in all those places hereinafter mentioned should throw all their zeal and energy into securing the progress of their disciples and that they should apply themselves to science as the necessity of the times demanded. He laid out for this exercise certain places chosen in such a manner that neither time nor distance nor poverty might any more serve as an excuse to the people. He desired therefore at Pavia and *under the superintendence of Dungal all students should assemble* from Milan, Brescia, Lodi, Bergamo, Novara, Vercelli, Tortona, Acqui, Genoa, Asti, and Como.[498] Thus we see what a responsible position Dungal occupied as head of the school of Pavia—the precursor of the famous university.

Dungal himself informs us that he was an Irishman in a poem in praise of Charlemagne which commences with these words: "These verses the Irish Exile (*exul Hibernicus*) sends to King Charles." He composed several other poems,[499] but that written to Charlemagne is his longest and best effort. The shorter poems display considerable taste but not much imagination. [500]

In 828 A.D. Dungal appeared in a controversy against Claudius, bishop of Turin, who had written against the veneration of images. It will be recalled that this Claudius was the learned and gifted Spaniard who described the Council of Italian bishops as a "council of asses" (*congregatio asinorum*). Against this formidable opponent Dungal was called upon to undertake the defence of the veneration of images. As Zimmer remarks, "these two learned adversaries, Claudius the Spaniard and Dungal the Irishman, who met on the soil of Lombardy, were the representatives of two countries—the only ones—which offered an asylum to Graeco-Roman culture at the beginning of the seventh century when it had declined in the West. Ireland was especially conspicuous in introducing it anew in the form of Christianity, principally into France, these efforts being made when civilization was at its lowest ebb and the country in its most degraded condition."[501]

We are not concerned here with the theological question at issue, but it may be remarked that Dungal's reply[502] shows that he was a man of wide culture, "accomplished too in sacred literature, and at the same time trained in grammatical laws and in the classical excellence of style as will readily appear to anyone who reads his writings."[503] Alzog informs us that the sophistical reasoning of Claudius was refuted by Jonas, bishop of Orleans, but much more ably by Dungal. He is styled an excellent theologian (*theologus excellans*) by a contemporary and Healy declares that Dungal's is the first and best work that was written on the subject.[504] The many quotations from Greek and Latin poets which occur in his reply to Claudius as well as in his epistle to Charlemagne prove that Dungal had a strong love for poetry and that he was well read in classic literature.[505] Thus we see that Dungal's education was built on a broad foundation, for he was distinguished as an astronomer and a theologian as well as a poet and a schoolmaster.

The last act of Dungal of which we have any record is his gift of books to the library of Bobbio.[506] Dungal is greatly praised by Muratori, Mabillon, Bellarmine and others for his learning and he was valued both in Italy and France for his varied attainments. Muratori, who published a catalogue[507] of the library of Bobbio, says that "Dungal carried into Italy the Scotic love of learning." Among the books which Dungal presented to Bobbio is one which was catalogued as Psalterium but named by Muratori as the *Antiphonary of Bangor*,[508] a book of hymns compiled expressly for the use of the monastic community of Bangor in Co. Down (Ireland). It is written in Latin, but it contains the strongest internal evidence of its Irish origin. On the strength of the evidence furnished by the fact that Dungal possessed this book many believe that Dungal himself was a pupil of Bangor. If so, we have in Dungal an excellent example of the type of education available in this famous monastic school in the ninth century.

SEDULIUS:

Under the Emperor Lothair 840–855 there was at Liège a colony of Irish teachers and writers of whom the best known is Sedulius, sometimes called Sedulius the Younger to distinguish him from the author of the *Carmen Paschale*. We have already referred to the fact that he was a distinguished poet[509] and a learned grammarian.[510] He is no less famous as a scribe[511] and as a writer on other subjects.

He wrote an important treatise on the theory of government entitled *De Rectoribus Christianis*.[512] This work was written at Liège probably about the year 855 A.D. It is in reality the first systematic contribution of the Middle Ages to the theory of political government and should rank in importance with St. Thomas's *De Regimine Principis*, with Colonna's *De Regimine Principum* and with Dante's *De Monarchia*.[513] As its latest editor Dr.

Hellman has remarked, if this work is not drawn from exclusively Irish sources, it is drawn at least from sources which were held in high esteem by Irish writers of the Carolingian Age. This Celtic conception of the duties of a Christian ruler is of very special interest to the student of mediæval political theories. Its sources are Christian and classical, its immediate object was the direction of a Frankish ruler (probably Lothair II.), the mind that conceived it was Celtic and here we have at the beginning of mediæval speculation a combination of forces and interests which went to make up the mediæval policy.[514]

Sedulius also wrote a commentary of Porphry's *Isagoge* (or Introduction to the Logic of Aristotle) for which the basis may have been the Greek text though the work was known to other Christian logicians only in the Latin translation.[515]

JOHANNES SCOTUS ERIUGENA (d. 877 A.D.):

This was by far the greatest Irish scholar of the ninth century. Indeed in many ways he was the most remarkable man of his age. Of his early life we have no details. He was born between the years 800–815 A.D. The general opinion of scholars is that he was born in Ireland as his name would indicate.[516] His learning itself is sufficient proof that he was educated in Ireland where alone he could get the benefit of such an education as the continental schools could no longer have furnished.[517]

About the middle of the ninth century he appeared at the court of King Charles the Bald by whom he was placed at the head of the Palace School. Though in some respects a worthless sovereign, Charles had at least one redeeming quality inasmuch as he emulated the example of his grandfather (Charlemagne) as a patron of letters. During his reign Irish scholars flocked in great numbers to the Continent. The monarch was fond of discussing knotty questions, and had a keen taste for the subtle disputations to which Irish dialectitians were devoted. Encouraged by his patronage the Irish monks emigrated in so great numbers to France that hostelries were built for their exclusive use.[518] The most eminent of these exiles[519] was Eriugena. No sooner had he reached France (c. 845 A.D.) than he was recognised as a remarkable linguist. Certain reputed works of Dionysius the Areopagite had been sent by Pope Paul I. to Pepin-le-Bref, and a splendid MS. of the mystical writings of the same author was subsequently presented to Louis the Pious by the Byzantine Emperor Michael. The works were of course in the Greek language and the greatest scholars of France were unable to translate them or to interpret their meaning.[520] The task was finally entrusted to Eriugena and he produced a satisfactory version. The learned Anastasius, the papal librarian, on reading the version of Eriugena, wrote to King Charles expressing his surprise that "a barbarian who hailed from the extreme confines of the world and who might have been deemed to be as ignorant of Greek as he was remote from civilization could have proved capable of comprehending the mysteries of the Greek tongue."[521]

Great as was his fame as a linguist his reputation as a philosopher is still greater. His philosophical speculations gave rise to discussions and controversies which even to the present day occupy the attention of the greatest thinkers. In his own day his views were nothing short of sensational. In addition to his translation of the Pseudo-Dionysius already referred to, Eriugena wrote a comprehensive philosophical work *De Divisione Naturae* [522] and a treatise *De Egressu et Regressu Animae ad Deum* of which only a fragment has come down to us.[523] He also contributed a treatise *De Predestinatione* to a theological controversy that was waged at that time. This work seems to have given offence to both parties. His *expositiones* or commentaries on the Pseudo-Dionysius are helpful in determining his philosophical views. He also wrote a commentary on the work of Martianus Capella, *De Nuptiis.*

It is as a philosopher, however, that Eriugena stands without an equal during his own time. It has been remarked that Eriugena appears to have been born subject to a strange fatality whereby men's opinions are always changing in regard to his philosophical views and the position to be assigned to him among philosophers. In the criticisms by Maurice Milman, Staudenmaier, St. Rene, Tailander, Christlieb, Hauréau, and Huber the view of each writer differs in some important respect from the views of the rest.[524] This is no less true of the criticism of living philosophers as the following quotations from two standard works on the *History of Philosophy* go to show. De Wülf writes: "In opposition to the majority of historians who describe Eriugena as the first of scholastics, we have no hesitation in calling him the first of anti-scholastics—and the most formidable at the present epoch. For his teaching propounds principles which are opposed to those of scholasticism and which form the starting-point of opposition movements."[525] Turner, on the other hand, says that Eriugena illustrates the many sidedness of the scholastic movement and proceeds as follows: "To classify as anti-scholastic whatever does not agree with the synthetic systems of the great masters of scholasticism is to break the line of continuous historical development which led through failure and partial success of Eriugena, Abelard, and other philosophers to the philosophy of the thirteenth century. Scholasticism in its final form is the outcome of the forces of Christian civilization which in different conditions and in less favourable circumstances produced the imperfect scholasticism of the period of beginning and the period of growth."[526]

Whatever may be the difference of opinion as to his place in a particular school or system of philosophy there can be but one as to his abilities as a scholar and an original thinker. According to De Wülf, "he must be regarded as one of the most striking personalities in the world of culture and learning in the early Middle Ages. He was far in advance of his time. While his contemporaries were only lisping in philosophy and his successors for centuries did little more than discuss a small number of disconnected philosophical questions, Eriugena in the ninth century worked out a complete philosophical synthesis. ... He was at once a scholar and a man of genius. What was altogether unique in the ninth century, he knew Greek, of which Alcuin scarcely knew the alphabet."[527] Turner while wishing to give a fair estimate of his place in history, warns us "not to let his brilliant qualities blind us to the enormity of his errors,"[528] but the same writer acknowledges that "he was without doubt the most learned man in his century, he was the first of the representatives of the new learning to attempt a system of constructive thought and he brought to his task a truly Celtic wealth of imagination and a spiritual force which lifted him above the plane of his contemporaries—mere epitomisers and commentators. His philosophy has all the charm which pantheism always possesses for a certain class of minds. It is subtle, vague, and poetic. When we come to examine its contents and method we find it dominated with the spirit of Neo-Platonism. Through the works of Pseudo-Dionysius and of Maximus, Eriugena made acquaintance with the teaching of Plotinus and Proculus; and when he came to construct his own system of thought he reproduced the essential traits of Neo-Platonic philosophy—pantheism, the doctrine of intuition, and universal redemption."

The sentence enunciated by Eriugena in his work on Predestination[529] as well as elsewhere that the true religion is also the true philosophy and *vice versa* is the theme of the entire scholastic philosophy. The consequences that follow from this maxim as enunciated that every doubt in regard to religious matters can be refuted by philosophy appeared so preposterous that a meeting of French clergy declared it to be insanity or blasphemy.[530] Religion is to Eriugena in its relations to philosophy what authority is to reason. In respect to rank reason precedes so also in respect to time, since what is taught by authority of the Fathers was discovered by them with the help of reason. The weak must naturally subject themselves to authority, but those who are less weak should be content with this all the less because the figurative nature of many expressions and further the undeniable accommodation exercised by the Fathers toward the understanding of the uneducated demand the use of reason as a corrective.[531] By reason is to be understood, however, not mere subjective opinion but the common thought which reveals itself in conversation when out of two reasons both are made one, each of the speakers becoming as it were the other.[532] While he maintains the priority of reason he is far from being a rationalist. Indeed he is more inclined to take side with the mystics—to belittle all reason unless it is illumined from on high. "Instead of rationalising theology, he would theosophise philosophy."[533]

Thus we see how Eriugena's philosophical speculations naturally became the basis for innumerable controversies which are still far from being definitely decided. Such controversies, however, have served a useful purpose in the history of philosophy. Eriugena assigns to philosophy the fourfold task: to divide, to define, to demonstrate, to analyse. This may be described as Eriugena's definition of the applicability of dialectic to philosophy and theology—a notion which, like the union of faith and science, is destined to develop in the subsequent growth of philosophy.[534]

Eriugena's knowledge of Greek, and fondness for Greek dogma and Alexandrine philosophy, led to the report that he made several journeys to Greece. But this conjecture has no foundation in fact.[535] Indeed the evidence we have collected with reference to the course of studies pursued in the Irish monastic schools would point to Ireland as the most likely place where he laid the foundations of his classical scholarship.

INFLUENCE OF IRISH SCHOLARSHIP:

The scope of Irish scholarship may in some measure be judged from the existing works of the great and better-known scholars mentioned in this and other chapters, but the precise influence of that scholarship is more difficult to estimate. It is only in very recent years that we have begun to realise how much native Irish literature and history owes to the Irish monastic schools. In the wider field of European scholarship there is still much room for investigation before we can confidently assign to Irish monastic scholarship its proper place. The superiority of Irish classical learning has been demonstrated and is now acknowledged by practically all scholars who have made an intensive study of the early Middle Ages.[536] But as a discerning historian has remarked, "what is of greatest significance is the fact that there reigned not only among the professed scholars but among the plain missionaries (whose name was legion) a classical spirit, a love of literature for its own sake and a keen delight in poetry. They brought imagination, they brought spiritual force to a world well nigh sunk in materialism. ... Their lighter productions show but one side of their Scottish nature. Their earnest single pursuit of learning in the widest sense attainable, their solid hard work as scholars is no less characteristic. Ireland was once the university not only of Northern England, but of the Frankish realm and if that progress was arrested after the fatal inroads of the Norsemen after 795 A.D. the seed which the Scots had sown in other lands grew to a nobler maturity than ever it reached on its own soil. ... Wherever they went they founded schools."[537]

Many other tributes to Irish monastic scholarship might be quoted. We have selected but two of these partly because of the weight of authority rightly associated with the author's name in each case and partly because they summarise the detailed evidence we have presented during the course of our study.

Turner says: "The Irish teachers left a lasting impression on their own and succeeding generations. Not only were they the chief teachers of grammar, poetry, astronomy, music, and geography when these branches had no other, or scarcely any other, representative on the continent of Europe, but they also profoundly influenced the course of mediæval thought in matters of philosophy and theology. Their elucidation of the Gospel of St. John and their commentaries on the Epistles of St. Paul formed a new school of exegesis. ... They introduced the Neo-Platonic point of view in metaphysical speculation and carried the art of dialectic to a higher point than it ever before attained. It is no exaggeration to say that they were the founders of scholasticism and that Ireland is the Ionia of mediæval philosophy."[538]

Zimmer too shows that the Irish missionaries were not merely the representatives of Christianity: "they were instructors in every branch of science and learning of the time, possessors and bearers of a higher culture than was at that time to be found anywhere on the Continent, and can surely claim to have been the pioneers,—to have laid the corner stone of western culture on the Continent."[539]

We have reached the end of our study. We have traced the rise, growth, and influence of the Irish monastic schools during the sixth, seventh, eighth, and ninth centuries. Their work and influence lasted for several centuries after the ninth, but during the period which we have investigated their influence was a dominant one in the history of European education. In the later centuries other factors contributed to the advancement of learning in Western Europe and while the Irish contribution was by no means negligible it was less distinctive, less significant, than during the period ending with the ninth century. If, then, we would form a correct idea of the position that Irish monastic schools occupy in the history of western culture, we have but to contrast the actual state of contemporary learning in the rest of Western Europe with that available in these schools; or to recall their large number and wide distribution, noting the liberal nature of the course of studies pursued therein and the generosity with which that learning was extended to all irrespective of race or social position. In either case we are driven to the conclusion that these schools were indeed the greatest educational factor of early mediæval times, that they were, in reality, the universities of the West, the lights that illumined the (so-called) Dark Ages.

BIBLIOGRAPHY

Sources

Adamnan, *Vita Sancti Columbae*, ed. Wm. Reeves, Dublin, 1857.

Aengus, *Feilire, Lebor Brec*, p. 23b; Book of Leinster, p. 373c: Book of Ballymote; ed. Whitley Stokes, Dublin, 1880.

Aethicus Istrius, *Cosmographia*, ed. Wuttke, Leipsig, 1854; extract in Wood-Martin's *Pagan Ireland*, p. 84.

Aileran, *Interpretatio Mystica Progenitorum Christi* in Migne's *Patrologia Latina* tomus 80.

Alcuin, *Opera Omnia*, ed. Froben in *Migne P. L.* tom. 100–101.

Aldhelm, *Opera*, ed. Dr. Giles in *Migne P. L.* tom. 89, col. 63.

Ancient Laws of Ireland, 5 vols., Dublin, 1865–1901.

Annals of the Four Masters, ed. John O'Donovan, Dublin, 1848–51.

Annals of Tighernach, ed. Whitley Stokes in *Revue Celtique*, vols. xvi.–xviii.

Annals of Ulster, ed. Wm. Hennessey and Bartholemy MacCarthy. 3 vols. Dublin, 1893, 1895, 1901.

Antiphonarium Benchorense, in O'Laverty's *Ecclesiastical History of Down and Connor*, vol. ii, p. xvii.

Bede, *Historia Ecclesiastica Gentis Anglorum*, English trans., revised by Sellar, London, 1884.

Best, R. I. Edition of *The Canonical Hours (from H. c. 17 T.C.D.)* in *Eriu*, iii, Dublin, 1907.

Best, R. I. Edition of *The Lebor Brecc Tractate* in *Miscellany to Kuno Meyer*, Halle, 1912.

Colgan, *Trias Thaumaturga* and *Acta Sanctorum* in Migne *Pat. Lat.* 53, 80, 87, 88.

Columba (Colm Cille), Writings in Reeve's *Adamnan* and *Liber Hymnorum*, ed. by Atkinson and Bernard, 2 vols. London, 1898.

Columbanus, *Writings* in *Migne P. L.* 80.

Confessio Sancti Patricii in *Liber Ardmachanus*, ed. by John Gwynn, also in *Tripartite Life*, ed. by Whitley Stokes.

Cormac's Glossary in *Three Glosses*, ed. Stokes, London, 1862.

Cummian Fada, *Paschal Epistle* in *Migne P. L.* tom. 87.

Dicuil, *De Mensura Orbis Terrarum*, Published by Walckenaer, Paris, 1807; Letronne, Paris, 1814; Gustav Parthey, Berlin, 1870.

Dungal, *Letter to Charlemagne explaining solar eclipse* in *Migne, P. L.*, tom. 105; M. G. H., Ep. IV, 570 ff.

Eriugena, *De Divisione Naturae*. In *Migne, P. L.* tom. 122.

Flann, Fina (King Ailfrid of Northumbria), *Poem in praise of Ireland* in *Lebor Brec*, p. 13, pub. in *Eriu*, viii. Dublin, 1911.

Facsimile of *Lebor Brec*, Dublin, 1876.

Facsimile of *Book of Leinster*, Dublin, 1880.

Facsimile of *Leabhar na h-Uidhre*, Dublin, 1870.

Facsimile of *Book of Ballymote*, Dublin, 1887.

Gwynn, John. *Book of Armagh*, edited by, Dublin, 1913.

Haddan and Stubbs, *Councils and Ecclesiastical Documents relating to Great Britain and Ireland*, 3 vols. Oxford, 1869.

Jonas, *Vita Sancti Columbani*, *Migne P. L.* 87, col. 1011 seq.

Liber Hymnorum, ed. by Robert Atkinson and J. H. Bernard. 2 vols. London, 1898.

Marianus Scottus, *Chronicle* in *Migne, P. L.* tom. 147, pp. 602–795.

Muirchu, *Memoir of St. Patrick*, in *Book of Armagh* and in *Tripartite Life*, II, p. 269.

Ogam Alphabet in *Book of Leinster*, p. 38.

Ozanam, Frederic, *Documents Inedits*, containing extracts from *Vita Sancti Donati Scotti Fesulani Episcopi*, Paris, 1897.

Planctus Caroli, by an Irish Monk of Bobbio, *Migne, P. L.*, 106.

Plummer, Charles. *Vitae Sanctorum Hiberniae*, 2 vols. Oxford, 1910.

Rule of St. Ailbe, ed. by Jos. O'Neill in *Eriu*, iii, pp. 92–109, from Brussels Codex, pp. 24 et seq.

Rule of St. Carthach, ed. by "Mac Eclaise" in *Irish Ecclesiastical Record*, May, 1910.

Rule of St. Comgall, ed. by John Strachan, in *Eriu*, i, 1904, in 3 MSS. Old Irish Metrical Rule not later than 800 A.D.

Riagul Chiarain, ed. by John Strachan, in *Eriu*, ii, pp. 227–228.

Riagul na Manach Liath, ibid., pp. 228–229.

Rule of St. Patrick (dealing with the relation between the Church and the Tribe), ed. by J. G. O'Keeffe, *Eriu*, i, pp. 216–224.

Riagul Cormaic Maic Cuilenain, Eriu, i, p. 192.

Rule of St. Mochuda, referred to in *Revue Celtique*, vol. 30, p. 113.

Regula cujusdam patris ad Monachos, et Regula cujus patris ad Virgines, Migne, P. L., 66, col. 987 seq.

Rules of St. Carthage and *of St. Maelruan* in *Irish Ecclesiastical Record*, vol. i.

Rule of St. Columba, in Skene's *Celtic Scotland*, ii, p. 508 seq.; also in Haddan and Stubbs' *Councils and Ecclesiastical Documents*, vol. ii, part i, p. 119. (Irish and English translation).

Regula Monarcherum of Columbanus in Migne, P. L., tom. 80.

Sedulius, *Writings*, in *Migne, P. L.*, tom. 103.

Sedulius, *De Rectoribus Christianis*, published by Cardinal Mai in *Specilegium Romanum*, also by Hellman, Munich, 1908.

Stokes and Strachan, *Thesaurus Palaeohibernicus*, 2 vols. Cambridge, 1903.

Stokes, Whitley, *Lives of the Saints from the Book of Lismore*. Irish text with English trans. Oxford, 1890.

Stokes, Whitley, *Tripartite Life of St. Patrick*, ed. by, in *Rolls Series*. 2 vols. London, 1887.

Tacitus, *Agricola*.

The Seven Liberal Arts, poem by an Irish monk of St. Gallen, in *Neues Archiv der Gesellschaft Geschichtskunde*. Vol. iv, pp. 627–629, Hanover, 1878.

Tirechan, *Notes on the Life of St. Patrick* in the *Book of Armagh*, and in *The Tripartite Life of St. Patrick*.

Ussher, *Veterum Epistolarum Hibernicarum Sylloge*, Dublin, 1847–1869.

Vitae Galli, Auctoribus, Wettino et Walafrido. Edited by Bruno Krusch in *Monumenta Germaniae Historiae*, SS. R. M. iv, pp. 229 seq.

Zimmer, Heinrich, *Glossae Hibernicae*. Berlin, 1881.

Secondary Authorities Consulted

Abbot, T. K., *Catalogue of MSS. in the Library of Trinity College, Dublin.* Dublin, 1900.

Abelson, Paul, *The Seven Liberal Arts, A Study in Medieval Culture*, New York, 1906.

Alzog, J., *Universal Church History*, 3 vols., Cincinnati, 1889.

Archivium Hibernicum, 6 vols., Dublin, 1912–1917.

Arnold, Matthew, *On the Study of Celtic Literature*, New York, 1913.

Baring-Gould, *Lives of the Saints*, London, 1897, 16 vols.

Barrett, Michael, *A Calendar of Scottish Saints*, Fort Augustus, 1904.

Bellesheim, Canon, *Geschichts der Katholischen Kirche Irland*, Mainz, 1890.

Bergin, Osborn, and Marstrander, Carl, *Miscellany to Kuno Meyer*, Halle, 1912.

Best, R. I., *Bibliography of Irish Philology and Irish Printed Literature*, Dublin, 1913.

Boswell, *An Irish Precursor of Dante*, London, 1908.

Brash, *Ogam-inscribed Monuments of the Gaedhil*, London, 1899.

Brooks, Stopford, *History of English Literature from the Beginning to the Norman Conquest*, London.

Bury, J. B., *The Life of St. Patrick and his Place in History*, London, 1905.

Cambridge History of English Literature, vol. i, Chaps. xii, xvi.

Catholic Encyclopedia, 15 vols., New York, 1907.

Concannon, (Mrs.) Helen, *Life of St. Columban, A Study of Ancient Irish Monastic Life*, Dublin, 1915.

Coffey, George, *New Grange and other Incised Monuments*, Dublin, 1912.

Coffey, George, *The Bronze Age in Ireland*, Dublin, 1913.

Coffey, George, *The Antiquities of Christian Ireland*, Dublin, 1910.

Conyngham, D. P., *Lives of Irish Saints and Martyrs*, New York, 1870–1885.

Cubberley, E. P., *Syllabus of Lectures on the History of Education*, New York, 1904.

Cyclopedia of Education, ed. by Paul Munroe, New York, 1914.

D'Alton, (Canon) J., *History of Ireland*, 4 vols., London, 1910.

Darmesteter, James, *English Studies*, London, 1896.

De Jubainville, H. d'Arbois, *Cours de Littérature celtique*, vol. i, Paris, 1883.

De Wülf, Maurice, *History of Medieval Philosophy*, English trans. by Dr. P. Coffey, Dublin, 1909.

Dictionary of Christian Biography, ed. Wm. Smith and Henry Wace, London, 1877. 4 vols.

Dictionary of National Biography, 25 vols., ed. by Leslie Stephen and Sidney Lee, New York, 1908, 1909, 1912.

Dill, (Sir) Samuel, *Roman Society in the Last Century of the Western Empire*, London, 1898.

Drane, Augusta Theodosia, *Christian Schools and Scholars*, 2 vols., London, 1867.

Dunn, Joseph, and Lennox, P. J., *Glories of Ireland* (a series of short essays by different contributors, with selected bibliographies), Washington, D.C., 1914.

Edmonds, (Rev.) Columba, *Irish Monks in Europe*, Article in *Glories of Ireland*, pp. 20–32.

Encyclopedia Britannica, 29 vols., Cambridge, 1910.

Esposito, Mario, *Knowledge of Greek in Ireland during the Middle Ages*, Article in *Studies*, Dublin, Dec., 1912.

Esposito, Mario, *Hiberno-Latin MSS. in Belgian Libraries*, Article in *Archivium Hibernicum*, vol. iii.

Esposito, Mario, *The Latin Writers of Medieval Ireland*, Article in *Hermathena*, vol. xiv., No. 33.

Esposito, Mario, *The Latin Writers of Medieval Ireland*, Article in *Irish Theological Quarterly*, vol. iv.

Erdman, *History of Philosophy*, English trans. by Williston S. Hough, New York, 1898.

Fowler, *Vita Sancti Columbae*, Oxford, 1894.

Flood, W. H. Grattan, *History of Irish Music*, Dublin 1913.

Flood, W. H. Grattan, *Irish Music*, Article in *Glories of Ireland*, pp. 71–77.

Flood, J. M., *Ireland: Its Saints and Scholars*, Dublin, 1917.

Friedel and Meyer, *La Vision de Tondale*, Paris, 1907.

Ginnell, Laurence, *The Brehon Laws*, London, 1894.

Ginnell, Laurence, *Laws in Ireland*, Article in *Glories of Ireland*.

Gougaud, Dom Louis, *Les Chrétientés celtiques*, Paris, 1911.

Green, John R., *The Making of England*, New York, 1882.

Gwynn, Aubrey, *Date of St. Columba's Birth*, Article in *Studies*, vol. viii., Dublin, Sept., 1918.

Gwynn, John, *Liber Ardmachanus*, edited by, Dublin, 1913.

Hauck, Albert, *Kirchengeschichte Deutschlands*, teil i, Leipsig, 1904.

Hauréau, B. *Les Ecoles d'Irlande*, chap. in *Singularités Historiques et Littéraires*, Paris, 1894.

Hauréau, B. *De La Philosophie Scholastique*, 2 vols., Paris, 1850.

Healy, John (Most Rev., D.D.), *Insula Sanctorum et Doctorum, Ireland's Ancient Schools and Scholars*, Dublin, 1902, 4th ed.

Healy, John (Most Rev., D.D.), *The Life and Writings of St. Patrick*, Dublin, 1905.

Herzog, *Realenzyklopadie für protestant Theologie* teil x. (Article by H. Zimmer, *Keltische Kirsche*).

Hull, Eleanor, *Early Christian Ireland*, London, 1905.

Hull, Eleanor, *A Text Book of Irish Literature*, 2 vols., Dublin, 1910.

Hull, Eleanor, *The Poem Book of the Gael*, London, 1918.

Hyde, Douglas, *A Literary History of Ireland*, London, 1906.

Hyde, Douglas, Article, *Education in Ireland*, in Munroe's *Cyclopedia of Education*.

Ireland Industrial and Agricultural, ed. Wm. Coyne, Dublin, 1900.

Jenner, Henry, Article, *Celtic Rite*, in *Catholic Encyclopedia*.

Joyce, P. W., *A Social History of Ireland*, 2 vols., Dublin, 1913.

Jusserand, J. J., *A Literary History of the English People*, vol. i, chap. i, *Celtic Literature*, New York, 1912.

Keating, Geoffrey, *History of Ireland*, 4 vols, Irish text and English translation, London, 1902–1914.

Keller, F., *Bilder und Schriftzuge in den irischen Manuscripten*, in *Mitteilungen des antiquarischen Gesellschaft*, English trans. and Remarks by Dr. Wm. Reeves, in *Ulster Journal of Archaeology*, vol. viii.

Ker, W. P., *Dark Ages*, London, 1904.

Lanigan, *Ecclesiastical History of Ireland*, Dublin, 1889.

Lindsey, W. M., *Early Irish Minuscule Script*, Oxford, 1910.

Leach, A. F., *Educational Charters and Documents*, 598–1909 A.D., Cambridge, 1911.

Leach, A. F., *The Schools of Medieval England*, London, 1915.

Macalister, R. A. S., *Studies in Irish Epigraphy*, 3 vols., Dublin, 1897, 1902, 1907.

Macalister, R. A. S., *Muiredach, Abbot of Monasterboice*, Dublin, 1914.

MacCaffrey, James (Rev.), *Pre-Patrician Christianity in Ireland*, Art. in *Irish Theological Quarterly*, Jan., 1906.

MacNeill, Eoin, Articles (in Irish) on *Ogham Writing*, in *Irisleabhar na Gaedhilge*, May–Nov., 1908.

MacNeill, Eoin, Article, *Ogam Inscriptions*, in *Transactions of the Royal Irish Academy*, July, 1909.

MacNeill, Eoin, *Where does Irish History Begin?* and other Articles, in *New Ireland Review*, Mar.–Dec., 1906.

MacNeill, Eoin, *An Irish Historical Tract*, dated 721 A.D., in *Transactions of the Royal Irish Academy*, xxviii, Dublin, 1910.

Manitius, Max, *Geschichte der Lateinischen Literatur des Mittelalters*, teil i, München, 1911.

Matthew, J. E., *The Literature of Music*, London, 1896.

McCormick, P. J. (Rev.), *Education of the Laity in the Early Middle Ages*, Washington, D.C., 1912.

McKenna, Jas. E. (Right Rev., D.D.), *Irish Art*, C.T.S. Publication, Dublin, 1910.

Meyer, Kuno, *Learning in Ireland in the Fifth Century*, Dublin, 1913.

Meyer, Kuno, *Ancient Irish Poetry*, London, 1911.

Meyer, Kuno, *Tocosca Cormaic*, Todd Lecture Series, Dublin, 1909.

Montalambert, Count de, *Les Moines d'Occident*, Paris, 1863.

Moran, Patrick (Cardinal), *Irish Saints in Great Britain*, Dublin, 1903.

Mullinger, Jas. Bass, *The Schools of Charles the Great*, New York (Reprint), 1911.

Munroe, Paul, *Text Book on the History of Education*, New York, 1914.

Munroe, Paul, *Cyclopedia of Education*, 4 vols., New York, 1914.

Nolan, T. P., *Irish Universities and Culture*, Dublin.

Norden, E., *Die Antike Kunstprosa von 6ten Jahrhundert vor Christus in die Zeit der Renaissance*, 2 vols., Leipsig, 1898.

O'Ceallaigh, Sean, *Saothar ar Sean i gCein*, Dublin, 1904.

O'Curry, Eugene, *Lectures on the MSS. Materials of Irish History*, Dublin, 1861.

O'Curry, Eugene, *Manners and Customs of the Ancient Irish*, London, 1873.

O'Donovan, John, *Tribes and Customs of Hy Fiachrach*, Irish Archaeological Society, Dublin, 1844.

O'Donovan, John, *Annals of the Four Masters*, ed. by, Dublin, 1851.

O'Donovan, John, *Irish Grammar*, Dublin.

O'Hanlon, John, *Lives of the Irish Saints*, 10 vols., Dublin, 1875.

O'Laverty, James, *Historical Account of the Diocese of Down and Connor*, Dublin, 1880.

O'Reilly, Edward, *Irish Writers*, Dublin, 1770.

O'Sullivan, Florence, *The Early Institutions of Ireland*, Dublin, 1902.

Ozanam, Frederic, *Documents Inedits*, Paris, 1897.

Ozanam, Frederic, *La Civilisation chrétienne chez les Francs* and *Études germaniques*, in *Oeuvres Completes*, Paris, 1872–81.

Paetow, Louis John, *The Arts Course in the Medieval University* with special reference to Grammar and Rhetoric. *University of Illinois, Studies*, iii, 7, 1910.

Plummer, Charles, *Vitae Sanctorum Hiberniae*, 2 vols. Valuable Introduction to vol. i, Oxford, 1910.

Poole, Reginald Lane, *Illustrations in the History of Medieval Thought*, London, 1884.

Quiggin, Edmund C., Article on *Ogam*, in *Encyclopedia Britannica*, vol. v, 1910.

Quiggin, Edmund C., *Irish Influence on English Literature*, Art. in *Glories of Ireland*.

Rashdall, Hastings, *Universities in Europe in the Middle Ages*, vol. i, Oxford, 1895.

Reeves, Wm., *Adamnan's Life of St. Columba*. Very valuable notes, Dublin, 1857.

Renan, J. E., *Poetry of the Celtic Races*, in *French and German Essayists* (World's Greatest Classics), New York, 1900.

Roessler, Charles, *Les Influence celtiques avant et après Columban*, Paris, 1906.

Roger, Maurice, *L'Enseignement des Lettres Classiques d'Ausone à Alcuin*, Scholarly, Paris, 1905.

Salmon, John, *The Ancient Irish Church*, Dublin, 1897.

Sandys, J. E., *History of Classical Scholarship*, 3 vols., 2nd edition, Cambridge, 1906–1908.

Sandys, J. E., *A Companion to Latin Studies*, Cambridge, 1913.

Schubiger, Père Anselm, *Die Sängerschule St. Gallens von Achten bis Zwolften Jahrhundert*, Einsiedeln, New York, 1858.

Sigerson, George, *Bards of the Gael and Gall*, 2nd ed., London, 1907.

Skene, W. F., *Celtic Scotland*, 3 vols., Edinburgh, 1876–80.

Stokes, Margaret, *Early Christian Art in Ireland*, Dublin, 1911.

Stokes, Margaret, *Six Months in the Appenines*, London, 1892.

Stokes, Margaret, *Three Months in the Forests of France*, London, 1895.

Stokes, George T., *Ireland and the Celtic Church*, London, 1886.

Stokes (and Strachan), *Thesaurus Palaeohibernicus*, 2 vols., Cambridge, 1903.

Stokes, Whitley, *The Tripartite Life of St. Patrick*, Rolls Series, 2 vols., London, 1887.

Stokes, Whitley, *Anecdota Oxoniensia, Lives of the Saints from Book of Lismore*, Oxford, 1890.

Sullivan, (Sir) Edward, *The Book of Kells*, Introduction and 34 coloured Plates, London, 1914.

Todd, James Henthorn, *St. Patrick, Apostle of Ireland*, Dublin, 1864.

Townsend, W. J., *The Great Schoolmen of the Middle Ages*, Reprint, New York, 1905.

Traube, Ludwig, *O Roma Nobilis*, Munich, 1891.

Traube, Ludwig, *Peronna Scottorum*, Munich, 1900.

Turner, Wm. (Right Rev., D.D.), *Irish Teachers in the Carolingian Revival*, a very scholarly and helpful article in *Catholic University Bulletin*, Washington, D.C., 1907, vol. xiii., pp. 382 et seq., 567 et seq.

Turner, Wm. (Right Rev., D.D.), *History of Philosophy*, Boston, 1903.

Ware, (Sir) James, *The Writers of Ireland*, in 2 Books, English translation by Walter Harris, Dublin, 1746.

Wattenbach, W., *Das Schriftwesen im Mittelalter*, Leipsig, 1875.; also, Article in *Ulster J. of Arch.*, vol. xii, Belfast, 1859.

West, A. F., *Alcuin and the Rise of Christian Schools*, New York, 1892.

Westwood, John, *The Book of Kells*, a lecture given in Oxford, November, 1886, Dublin, 1887.

Warren, F. E., *Liturgy and Ritual of the Celtic Church*, Oxford, 1881.

White, S. J., *Apologia*.

Wood-Martin, W. G., *Pagan Ireland*, A Hand Book of Pre-Christian Antiquities, London, 1895.

Zeuss, J. C., *Grammatica Celtica*, Berlin, 1871.

Zimmer, Heinrich, *The Celtic Church in Britain and Ireland*. English translation by Miss A. Zimmer of Article in *Realenzyklopadie für prot. Theologie* (Hertzog), teil x, London, 1902.

Zimmer, Heinrich, *Pelagius in Ireland*, Berlin, 1901.

Zimmer, Heinrich, *Ueber Bedeutung des irischen Elements für die Mittelliche Kultur* (Preuss. Jahrbuch, lix, 1887), English translation by Miss Edmands under the title *Irish Element in Medieval Culture*, New York, 1891. A most interesting essay containing a wonderful accumulation of facts with reference to Irish schools and scholars on the Continent, but unfortunately without a bibliography, or references.

The names of a few additional authorities consulted or cited appear in the footnotes.

FOOTNOTES:

[1] Hyde, Douglas, *Literary History of Ireland*, p. 122.

[2] Cited by George Coffey, *Bronze Age in Ireland*, pp. 2, 3.

[3] Coffey, George, *op. cit.* pp. 6–99.

[4] Joyce, Patrick W., *Social History of Ireland*, I., p. 556.

[5] Coffey, George, *op. cit.* p. 2.

[6] Coffey, George, *New Grange and other Incised Tumuli*, p. 62.

[7] Coffey, George, *The Bronze Age in Ireland*, pp. 2, 27.

[8] O'Donovan, John, *Annals of the Four Masters*, I., p. 132.

[9] Joyce, P. W., *op. cit.* I., p. 14.

[10] Ginnell, Laurence, *Article on the Brehon Laws*, in the *Encyclopædia Britannica*, IV., p. 488.

[11] Quoted by Douglas Hyde in *A Literary History of Ireland*, p. 134.

[12] *Liber Ardmachanus* or *Book of Armagh*, edited by John Gwynn, p. 9.

[13] Stokes, Whitley, *Tripartite Life of St. Patrick*, II., p. 284.

[14] Joyce, Patrick W., *Social History of Ireland*, I., p. 402.

[15] The Brehon Laws have been edited and translated and published in five volumes with the title *The Ancient Laws of Ireland*.

[16] Joyce, P. W., *op. cit.* I., p. 403, who cites Petrie's *Tara*, p. 38.

[17] See Chapter IV. for a brief account of the Irish Lay Schools.

[18] See under *Prosody*, O'Donovan's *Irish Grammar*.

[19] See Joyce, P. W., *Social History of Ireland*, I., p. 316.

[20] *Cosmographia Aethici Istri*, edited by H. Wuttke, Leipsic, 1854.
Cited by Joyce, P. W., *op. cit.* I., p. 404.
Cited by Meyer, Kuno, *Learning in Ireland*, p. 11.
Cited by Wood-Martin, *Pagan Ireland*, p. 84.

[21] See Joyce, P. W., *Social History of Ireland*, I., p. 397.

[22] For the geographical distribution of Ogam inscriptions see Coffey, George, *Guide to Celtic Antiquities*, pp. 101–106.

[23] Perhaps the best division of the Irish language into periods
is that given by Eoin MacNeill in *Irisleabhar na Gaedhilge*, May, 1908.
Pre-Ogam, before 300 A.D. Ogam, c. 300(?)–700(?) A.D.
The Old Irish of the MSS. from 600(?)–1000(?) A.D.
Middle Irish, 1000–1500 A.D. Modern Irish, 1500–Present Day.
During the present study we shall frequently use the words Old Irish
to connote the Period including the 7th, 8th, and 9th centuries.

[24] Quiggin, E. C., *Article on Ogam* in *Encyclopædia Britannica*, vol. v., pp. 622–623.

[25] Joyce, P. W., *op. cit.* I., pp. 398–399.

[26] MacNeill, Eoin, Article *Irish Ogam Inscriptions* in the *Proceedings of the Royal Irish Academy*, July 1909.

[27] Bury, J. B., *Life of St. Patrick*, p. 10.

[28] Sigerson, George, *Bards of the Gael and Gall*, Introduction, p. 1.

[29] Meyer, Kuno, *Ancient Irish Poetry*, pp. 8, 9.

[30] De Jubainville, H. d'Arbois, *Literature Celtique*, I., p. 1.

[31] Meyer, Kuno, *Learning in Ireland in the Fifth Century*, p. 1.

[32] See Introduction to the *Book of Armagh*, ed. by John Gwynn; also Hyde, Douglas, *Literary History of Ireland*, pp. 137–139.

[33] Zimmer, Heinrich, *Celtic Church in Britain and Ireland*, p. 31.

[34] Bury, J. B., *Life of St. Patrick*, p. 206.

[35] Stokes, Whitley, *Tripartite Life of St. Patrick*, I., p. cxxxv.

[36] Bury, J. B., *Life of St. Patrick*, p. 206.

[37] Stokes, Whitley, *Tripartite Life of St. Patrick*, I., 112, 138, 190–322, 326, 327, 328.

[38] Joyce, P. W., *Social History of Ireland*, I., p. 439. See illustration.

[39] *Würzburg Codex*, 33 c. 13.

[40] Stokes, Whitley, *op. cit.* I., p. xviii.

[41] Roger, M., *L'Enseignement des Lettres Classiques*, p. 222.

[42] Meyer, Kuno, *Learning in Ireland, in the Fifth Century*, p. 1.

[43] Meyer, Kuno, *op. cit.* p. 5.

[44] De Jubainville H. d'Arbois, *Cours de littérature celtique*, I., p. 369.

[45] Meyer, Kuno, *op. cit.* pp. 5, 6.

[46] Gwynn, John, *Book of Armagh*, f. 22 b. 2; also Stokes, Whitley, *Tripartite Life of St. Patrick*, II., pp. 357–380.

[47] Translated from Latin of *Tripartite Life*, II., pp. 360–361.

[48] Zimmer, H., *Sitzungsberichte der köngl. preuss. Akademie*, 1909, p. 562, cited by Meyer, Kuno, *op. cit.* p. 5.

[49] Meyer, Kuno, *ibid.*

[50] Colganus, *Acta Sanctorum Hiberniae*, XI., p. 375, cited by Hauréau, B., *Singularités Historiques et Littéraires*, pp. 2, 3.

[51] Power, Patrick, *Lives of SS. Declan and Mochuda*, p. xix.

[52] Tacitus, *Agricola*, Chapter XXIV.

[53] *Ibid.*

[54] See Coffey, George, *Archæological Evidence for the Intercourse of Gaul with Ireland before the First Century* in *Proceedings of the Royal Irish Academy*, 1910, pp. 96–106; Greene, Alice S., *Trade Routes of Ireland* in her *Old Irish World*, pp. 63–99.

[55] Meyer, Kuno, Article, *Gauls in Ireland* in *Eriu*, IV., p. 208.

[56] Warren, J. B., *Liturgy and Ritual of the Celtic Church*, p. 35.

[57] Healy, John, *Ireland's Ancient Schools and Scholars*, pp. 29–39; Warren, J. B., *op. cit.* p. 35.

[58] Healy, John, *op. cit.* p. 32.

[59] Sigerson, George, *Bards of the Gael and Gall*, p. 45.

[60] Sigerson, George, *op. cit.* pp. 45–48.

[61] Healy, John, *op. cit.* p. 39, where St. Jerome is cited.

[62] Meyer, Kuno, *Learning in Ireland*, p. 8.

[63] Healy, John, *op. cit.* p. 40.

[64] Healy, John, *op. cit.* p. 41.

[65] Meyer, Kuno, *op. cit.*; also Warren, F. E., *Liturgy and Ritual of the Celtic Church*, p. 35.

[66] Article, *Ireland* in the *Catholic Encyclopædia*, VIII., p. 117.

[67] *Op. cit.* VIII., p. 116.

[68] MacCaffrey, James, Article, *Rome and Ireland: Pre-Patrician Christianity*, in *Irish Theological Quarterly*, I., p. 53.

[69] Baeda, *Historia Ecclesiasticae Gentis Anglorum*, Liber I., Cap. 13.

[70] For a discussion of the ancient use of the words *Scotia* and *Scot* see Skene's *Celtic Scotland*, I., Introduction, p. 9.

[71] Bury, J. B., *Life of St. Patrick*, pp. 212–213.

[72] Bury, J. B., *op. cit.* p. 217.

[73] Joyce, P. W., *op. cit.* I., p. 323.

[74] Hyde, Douglas, *Literary History of Ireland*, pp. 243–251.

[75] Plummer, Carolus, *Vitae Sanctorum Hiberniae*, I., Intro., 129–188.

[76] Hyde, Douglas, *op. cit.* pp. 134–135.

[77] De Jubainville, H. d'Arbois, *Littérature Celtique*, I., 137.

[78] Todd, W. H., *Life of St. Patrick*, pp. 88, 89, contains a copy of *Catalogus SS. Hiberniae Secundum Diversa Tempora.*

[79] Article on *Monasticism* signed E. C. B. (E. C. Butler) in the *Encyclopædia Britannica*, XVIII., p. 687.

[80] *Ibid.*

[81] Healy, John, *Ireland's Ancient Schools and Scholars*, p. 93.

[82] Bund, Willis, *Celtic Church in Wales*, 1897, cited by G. P. Huddleston in Article on *Irish Monasticism* in the *Catholic Encylopædia*, X., p. 473.

[83] See Bibliography, *Sources — Rules.*

[84] See Bibliography, *Lives of Irish Saints.*

[85] Warren, F. E., *The Liturgy and Ritual of the Celtic Church*, pp. 54–55.

[86] *Catholic Encyclopædia, op. cit.*

[87] *Catalogus SS. Hiberniae Secundum Diversa Tempora*, published in Todd, W. H., *Life of St. Patrick*, pp. 88–89.

[88] Bury, J. B., *op. cit.* p. 39 *seq.* Healy, John, *op. cit.* p. 93.

[89] Plummer, Charles, *Vitae Sanctorum Hiberniae*, p. cxxiv.

[90] Plummer, Charles, *op. cit.* p. cxxv.

[91] *Ibid.*

[92] Plummer, Charles, *op. cit.* I., p. cxxvi.

[93] Healy, John, *op. cit.* p. 199.

[94] Joyce, *Social History of Ireland*, I., 322.

[95] Todd, W. H., *op. cit.* p. 99; Healy, J. *op. cit.* pp. 107–108.

[96] Stokes, Whitley, *Felire of Aengus*, p. 118.

[97] Joyce, P. W., *op. cit.* I., 323.

[98] Reeves, Wm., *Adamnan's Life of St. Columba*, pp. 276–298.

[99] Healy, John, *op. cit.* p. 61.

[100] Joyce, P. W., *op. cit.* I., p. 321.

[101] *Op. cit.* I., 323.

[102] Nolan, Thomas, *Irish Universities and Culture*, p. 11.

[103] Conyngham, D. P., *Lives of Irish Saints and Martyrs*, pp. 537–544.

[104] Murray, Rev. L. P., Article in *Louth Archæological Journal*, I., pp. 22–36.

[105] In *Proceedings of the Royal Irish Academy*, VI., p. 106 *seq.* cited by Warren, F. E., *op. cit.* p. 16.

[106] White, *Apologia*, p. 24 cited by Nolan, P., *op. cit.* p. 18.

[107] Stokes, Margaret, *Three Months in the Forests of France*, p. 254–5.

[108] Green, J. R., *The Making of England*, pp. 277–8.

[109] Reeves, Wm., *Adamnan*, pp. 290–303.

[110] Todd, W. H., *Wars of the Gael and Gall*, Rolls Series, p. 39.

[111] Zimmer, H., *Irish Element in Mediæval Culture*, p. 49.

[112] Reeves, Wm., *Adamnan's Life of St. Columba*, pp. 276–298.

[113] Moran, Patrick, *Irish Saints in Great Britain*, 77 *seq.*

[114] Edmonds, Columba, Article in *Glories of Ireland*, p. 21.

[115] Especially Skene, W., *Historians of Scotland*, VI., p. xlix. Also in *Celtic Scotland*, III.

[116] Warren, F. E., *Liturgy and Ritual of the Celtic Church*, p. 14.

[117] See, however, Green, J. R., *The Making of England*, p. 276 *seq.*; Brooke, Stopford, *History of English Literature from the Beginning to the Norman Conquest*, Chap. I., II., III.; also *Cambridge History of English Literature*, I., Chap. II., pp. 13, 14, 15, 16.

[118] Warren, F. E., *op. cit.* p. 16.

[119] Warren, F. E., *ibid.;* Sandys, *History of Classical Scholarship*, I., p. 442; Meyer, Kuno, *Learning in Ireland*, p. 12.

[120] Warren, F. E., *ibid.;* Roger, *op. cit.* 400; also Hauck, Albert, *Kirchengeschichte Deutschlands*, I., pp. 282 *seq.*

[121] Warren, F. E., *op. cit.* p. 16; Stokes, Margaret, *Six Months in Apennines*, pp. 96–97.

[122] Warren, F. E., *op. cit.* p. 3.

[123] Warren, F. E., *op. cit.* pp. 63–64; also Haddan and Stubbs' *Councils and Ecclesiastical Documents of Great Britain and Ireland*, I., p. 152.

[124] Warren, F. E., *op. cit.* p. 3.

[125] Reeves, Wm., *op. cit.* p. 350.

[126] Bede, *Ecclesiastical History of England*, Bohn's Edition, pp. 371–2.

[127] Reeves, Wm., *op. cit.* p. 350.

[128] Plummer, Charles, *op. cit.* I., p. cxxiii.

[129] Healy, John, *op. cit.* pp. 236–237.

[130] *Catholic Encyclopædia*, III., p. 404.

[131] Bede, *Ecclesiastical History of England*, Book III., Bohn's Ed.; Bede, *op. cit.* Book III., 26–28, Book IV., 12, 21, 23; Plummer's Edition cited by Roger, *op. cit.* 823–4.

[132] Roger, *ibid.*

[133] Healy, John, *op. cit.* pp. 236, 237.

[134] Joyce, P. W., *op. cit.* I., p. 460.

[135] Green, J. R., *The Making of England*, p. 276.

[136] Reeves, Wm., *op. cit.* p. 342.

[137] Reeves, Wm., *op. cit.* See table opposite p. 342.

[138] Reeves, Wm., *Adamnan*, pp. 342, 343; Skene, W., *Celtic Scotland*, II., pp. 61, 62. The monastic organization here described applies especially to Iona, but may be considered as typical not only of Columban monasteries but of Irish monasteries in general.

[139] Reeves, Wm., *op. cit.* p. 365; Healy, John, *op. cit.* p. 98.

[140] Skene, Wm., *Celtic Scotland*, II., p. 44.

[141] Skene, Wm., *op. cit.* p. 42.

[142] See *Annals of the Four Masters*, I., pp. 399, 410, 420, 442, 458, 470.

[143] Joyce, P. W., *op. cit.* I., p. 389.

[144] *Ancient Laws of Ireland*, V., p. 123.

[145] Todd, W. H., *Life of St. Patrick*, p. 16.

[146] Joyce, P. W., *op. cit.* I., p. 381.

[147] Healy, John, *op. cit.* p. 104.

[148] Joyce, P. W., *op. cit.* I., p. 381.

[149] Todd, W. H., *op. cit.* p. 160.

[150] Healy, John, *op. cit.* pp. 104, 105.

[151] Healy, John, *ibid.;* Plummer, Charles, *op. cit.* I., p. cxiv.

[152] *Ancient Laws of Ireland*, III., 13, 15, 29.

[153] Joyce, P. W., *op. cit.* I., pp. 318, 382.

[154] Joyce, P. W., *op. cit.* I., pp. 378, 379, 380.

[155] *Ancient Laws of Ireland*, III., pp. 33, 39.

[156] The relation between the Irish Church and the State is very ably yet concisely treated in a pamphlet by Rev. James F. Cassidy, St. Paul, Minnesota, entitled *"The Irish Church as an Element in Irish Nationality"* whose thesis is cited here.

[157] Joyce, P. W., *op. cit.* I., p. 382.

[158] Healy, John, *op. cit.* p. 94; Stokes, Whitley, *Tripartite Life of St. Patrick*, I., p. 236.

[159] Plummer, Charles, *op. cit.* I., p. xcviii.

[160] Joyce, P. W., *op. cit.* I., 365.

[161] Reeves, Wm., *Adamnan*, pp. 24, 143.

[162] Concannon, Helen, *The Life of St. Columban*, p. 145.

[163] Stokes, W., *op. cit.* p. 236; Reeves, Wm., *op. cit.* pp. 357–361.

[164] Reeves, Wm., *ibid.;* Healy, John, *op. cit.* pp. 94–96.

[165] Warren, F. E., *op. cit.* p. 17.

[166] Warren, F. E., *op. cit.* p. 17; Joyce, P. W., *op. cit.* I. 1. 409.

[167] See Bibliography, *Rules*.

[168] *Op. cit. Lives of Saints.*

[169] Columbanus, *Regula Monachorum*, C. III., cited by Concannon, Helen, *Life of St. Columban*, p. 68.

[170] Reeves, Wm., *Adamnan's Vita Sancti Columbae*, p. 348.

[171] Concannon, Helen, *op. cit.* p. 69.

[172] *Ibid.*

[173] Reeves, Wm., *op. cit.* p. 355.

[174] Concannon, Helen, *ibid.*

[175] *Ibid.*

[176] McAlister, R. S., *Muiredach, Abbot of Monasterboice*, p. 63.

[177] The number of Canonical Hours vary in different Rules; some give *six*, others *seven*; the Bangor usage was *eight*. See notes by R. I. Best on *Tractate on the Canonical Hours* edited from the *Lebor Brecc* in *Miscellany to Kuno Meyer.*

[178] See Concannon, Helen, *op. cit.* pp. 58, 67; Plummer, I., cxvii.

[179] MacAlister, R. S., *Muiredach, Abbot of Clonmacnoise*, p. 63.

[180] See above *Means of Support.*

[181] Concannon, Helen, *op. cit.* p. 75.

[182] Healy, J., *op. cit.* p. 104.

[183] Published in Skene's *Celtic Scotland*, II., p. 509.

[184] Adamnan, *Vita S. Columbae*, Reeves Edition, p. 9.

[185] Stokes and Strachan, *Thesaurus Palaeohibernicus*, I., pp. 3–483 for *Glosses on Psalms*; O'Hanlon, John, *Lives of Irish Saints*, VI., p. 286 for story of St. Columba.

[186] Reeves, Wm., *Adamnan's Life of St. Columba*, pp. 20, 22, 36, 43, 49.

[187] Reeves, W., *op. cit.* pp. 343, 344.

[188] Healy, John, *op. cit.* p. 103.

[189] Concannon, Helen, *op. cit.* pp. 186–191.

[190] Reeves, Wm., *op. cit.* pp. 343, 344.

[191] Joyce, P. W., *op. cit.* I., 29, 25, 330, 332; II., 166, 167, 168, 483.

[192] Reeves, Wm., *op. cit.* pp. 343, 344.

[193] For translations of Early Irish Nature Poetry see Sigerson, G., *Bards of the Gael and Gall*; Meyer, Kuno, *Old Irish Poetry*; Hull, Eleanor, *Poem Book of the Gael*.

[194] Healy, John, *op. cit.* pp. 102, 103.

[195] Zimmer, H., *Irish Element in Mediæval Culture*, p. 102.

[196] Johnson, Samuel (Dr.), in a letter to Charles O'Connor published in O'Reilly's *Irish Writers*, pp. i., ii. Also cited in Article *Dr. Johnson and Ireland* in *Irish Monthly*, XLVI., 538, p. 211.

[197] Joyce, P. W., *Social History of Ireland*, I., 408.

[198] Hyde, Douglas, *Literary History of Ireland*, p. 241.

[199] Hull, Eleanor, *Text Book of Irish Literature*, I., 189.

[200] Joyce, P. W., *Social History of Ireland*, I., pp. 418, 419.

[201] O'Curry, Eugene, *Manners and Customs*, I., p. 78.

[202] O'Donovan, John, *Tribes and Customs of Hy Many*, pp. 79, 167.

[203] Joyce, P. W., *op. cit.* I., 417.

[204] See also *Catalogue of Irish MSS. in Trinity College, Dublin*, pp. 285–402, 530–535; *The Bibliography of Irish Philology and Irish Printed Literature*, edited by R. I. Best, pp. 1–307.

[205] Reeves, Wm., *Adamnan*, pp. 103, 107.

[206] *Op. cit.*, pp. 79–80.

[207] Meyer, Kuno, *Old Irish Poetry*. See several examples; also *Thesaurus Palaeohibernicus*, II., pp. 290, 293, 294, 296.

[208] De Jubainville, H. d'Arbois, *Littérature Celtique*, I., 384.

[209] Joyce, P. W., *op. cit.* I., pp. 418, 419; Hull, E., *op. cit.* I., 189.

[210] Joyce, P. W., *op. cit.* I., 417.

[211] O'Curry, Eugene, *Manners and Customs*, I., 92. *MS. Materials*, p. 50.

[212] The Irish word *fithcheal* is usually translated *chess*.

[213] *Ancient Laws of Ireland*, II., 349. Also pp. 153, 1616.

[214] Joyce, P. W., *op. cit.* I., pp. 418, 426. For *Fosterage*, see II., p. 14.

[215] Joyce, P. W., *op. cit.* I., pp. 418, 426.

[216] Healy, John, *op. cit.* p. 132.

[217] Healy, John, *op. cit.* p. 211.

[218] Stokes, Whitley, *Lives of the Saints from the Book of Lismore.*

[219] Plummer, C., *op. cit.* I., p. cxv.; Joyce, *op. cit.* I., 440, p. 251.

[220] Concannon, Helen, *op. cit.* p. 10.

[221] *Op. cit.* pp. 24, 25.

[222] De Jubainville, H. d'Arbois, *La Civilization des Celtes*, p. 109.

[223] Warren, F. E., *op. cit.* p. 14; Moran, Patrick, *Irish Saints in Great Britain*, pp. 248, 240. Montalambert, Conte de, *Les Moines d'Occident*, IV., p. 62.

[224] For the influence of the Irish monks on early English poetry, see Brooke, Stopford, *History of English Literature from the Beginning to the Norman Conquest*, Chapters i., ii., iii. Also *Cambridge History of English Literature*, I., pp. 13–16.

[225] Joyce, P. W., *op. cit.* I., p. 410.

[226] *Zeitschrift für Celtische Philologie*, II., p. 137.

[227] Stokes, Whitley, *Lives of the Saints*, line 4128.

[228] Plummer, C., *Vitae Sanctorum Hiberniae*, I., p. cxv.

[229] Todd, J. H., *Life of St. Patrick.* See *Catalogus Sanctorum Hiberniae Secundum Diversa Tempora*, printed on pp. 88, 89.

[230] *Book of Leinster*, p. 373; *Lebor Brec*, p. 23 b; edited Stokes, Whitley, *Royal Irish Academy MSS. Series*, 1880.

[231] Meyer, Kuno, *Learning in Ireland*, p. 24.

[232] Petrie, George, *Christian Inscriptions*, II., p. xiv.

[233] Joyce, P. W., *op. cit.* I., p. 413.

[234] Plummer, C., *op. cit.* I., xiv.

[235] *Epistolas* in *Monumenta Germaniae Historiae*, Epistola III.; *Epistolas Merovingi et Carolingi Aevi*, I., p. 231.

[236] Bede, *Ecclesiastical History of England*, Bk. III., Chap. xxvii., Bohn's English Translation.

[237] Healy, John, *op. cit.* pp. 530–532.

[238] Petrie, George, *Round Towers*, p. 355. O'Curry, E., *Manners & C.*, p. 38.

[239] Moran, Patrick, *Irish Saints in Great Britain*, pp. 219–223.

[240] Published in *Eriu*, VIII. text, p. 67, translation p. 74.

[241] Hyde, Douglas, *op. cit.* p. 221.

[242] Roger, M. L., *Enseignement des lettres classiques*, p. 410.

[243] Moran, Patrick, *op. cit.* p. 253.

[244] Quoted from Zimmer, H., *Irish Element in Mediæval Culture*, p. 32.

[245] Bede, *op. cit.* Book V., Chap. IX., X.

[246] Bede, *op. cit.* III., vii.

[247] Bede, *op. cit.* IV., ii.

[248] See Migne's *Patrologia Latina*, Tomus 89, col. 3.

[249] Zimmer, *op. cit.* p. 42.

[250] Meyer, *Learning in Ireland*, p. 13.

[251] Joyce, P. W., *op. cit.* I., p. 412.

[252] Healy, John, *op. cit.* pp. 272, 273.

[253] Turner, Wm., *Catholic University Bulletin*, XIII., p. 388, 1907.

[254] Roger, M., *op. cit.* p. 314.

[255] Published in Migne, *Patrologia Latina*, Tomus, 142; *Alcuini Epistola*, 3; Ussher, *Sylloge: Epistola 18*.

[256] *Dictionary of National Biography*, Article on *Colchu* by T. O. (Thomas Orpen), XI., pp. 259, 260.

[257] *Dictionary of National Biography*, XI., *loc. cit.* pp. 259, 260.

[258] Healy, John, *op. cit.* pp. 272–273.

[259] Plummer, Charles, *Vitae Sanctorum Hiberniae*, I., p. cxv.; Joyce, P. W., *Social History of Ireland*, I., p. 440.

[260] Stokes, Whitley, *Lives of the Saints from the Book of Lismore*, p. 173.

[261] Joyce, P. W., *op. cit.* I., 437.

[262] O'Curry, Eugene, *Manners and Customs of the Ancient Irish*, I., p. 149; Healy, John, *Ireland's Ancient Schools and Scholars*, p. 435.

[263] Bede, *Ecclesiastical History of England*, Chapter xxvii., Bohn's Ed.

[264] Stokes, Whitley, *op. cit.* p. 172.

[265] See Joyce. P. W., *op. cit.* I., 439 for illustration of alphabet engraved on a large stone in Kilmakedar in Co. Kerry.

[266] Plummer, Charles, *op. cit.* I., p. cxv.

[267] See Stokes and Strachan, *Thesaurus Palaeohibernicus*, I., pp. 3–481.

[268] Joyce, P. W., *op. cit.* I., pp. 482–484.

[269] Coffey, George, *Guide to Celtic Antiquities of the Christian Period,* see illustration, p. 99.

[270] Joyce, P. W., *op. cit.* I., p. 438.

[271] Stokes and Strachan, *Thesaurus Palaeohibernicus,* I., p. 567; Zimmer, H., *Glossae Hiberniae*, p. 69, Note 7.

[272] Stokes and Strachan, *op. cit.* I., p. 516.

[273] Joyce, P. W., *op. cit.* p. 440.

[274] *Book of Leinster*, p. 135; *Rawlinson* MS. B. 502, p. 77, edited by Kuno Meyer; *Proceedings of the Royal Irish Academy*, 1883, pp. 219–252, edited and translated by Thomas Olden; cited by *Revue Celtique*, V., p. 192.

[275] Macalister, R. A. S., *Muiredach, Abbot of Clonmacnoise*. See Map on Plate I., opposite p. 12.

[276] Traube, Ludwig, *O Roma Nobilis*, p. 58.

[277] Concannon, Helen, *Life of St. Columban*, pp. 41–42.

[278] Stokes and Strachan, *op. cit.* II., p. xix., and for Glosses see *op. cit.* II., pp. 49–232.

[279] Joyce, P. W., *op. cit.* I., pp. 430–431.

[280] Joyce, P. W., *op. cit.* I., p. 432.

[281] See Macalister, R. A. S., *Muiredach*, p. 65, for a collection of these fragmentary marginalia.

[282] Joyce, P. W., *op. cit.* I., 483.

[283] Reeves, Wm., *Adamnan*, Preface, lviii.

[284] *Ancient Laws of Ireland*, III., p. 89.

[285] Sullivan, Sir Edward, *The Book of Kells*, p. 24.

[286] Sullivan, Sir Edward, *op. cit.* p. 25.

[287] Or the juice of "green skinned holly," Meyer, Kuno, *Ancient Irish Poetry*, p. 87.

[288] Keller, Ferdinand, *Ulster Journal of Archæology*, Old Series, VIII., p. 222.

[289] Stokes, Margaret, *Early Christian Ireland*, Article ix.

[290] See Abbot's *Reproduction of the Book of Kells*, Plate xxxiv.; also reproduced in Sir Arthur Sullivan's *The Book of Kells*.

[291] Joyce, P. W., *op. cit.* I., p. 480, illustration i., 481.

[292] Joyce, P. W., *op. cit.* I., pp. 477–478.

[293] See Chapter III.; also *Four Masters*, I., passim.

[294] Reeves, Wm., *Adamnan*, Preface, pp. xxi.–xxii.

[295] Sandys, J. E., *Companion of Latin Studies*, Article on *Palaeography* by Sir Edward Maude Thompson, pp. 780–781.

[296] Keller, F., *Ulster Journal of Archæology*, O.S. VIII., p. 223.

[297] Keller, F., *Bilder und Schriftzuge*, Zurich, 1851, English translation *Ulster Journal of Archæology*, VIII., pp. 210–291.

[298] Lindsey, W. M., *Early Irish Minuscule Script*, Oxford, 1910.

[299] Sandys, J. E., *Companion of Latin Studies*, p. 281.

[300] Zimmer, H., *Irish Element in Mediæval Culture*, pp. 121–124.

[301] Zimmer, H., *op. cit.* p. 120.

[302] Hull, Eleanor, *Early Christian Ireland*, p. 270.

[303] Joyce, P. W., *op. cit.* I., p. 488.

[304] Coffey, George, *Guide to the Antiquities of Christian Ireland.* See illustration, p. 50.

[305] Joyce, P. W., *op. cit.* I., p. 489.

[306] Hull, Eleanor, *Early Christian Ireland*, p. 271.

[307] Hull, E., *ibid.* Sandys in his *History of Classical Scholarship*, I., p. 453 gives 666 as the number of volumes.

[308] See Muratori, *Antiquitates Italiae*, fol. ed. I., *Dissert.* 43, pp. 493.

[309] Stokes, Margaret, *Six Months in the Appenines*, pp. 296–7.

[310] Sandys, J. E., *op. cit.* I., p. 453; Hull, Eleanor, *op. cit.* p. 272.

[311] Zimmer, H., *Irish Element in Mediæval Culture*, p. 116.

[312] Sandys, J. E., *op. cit.* I., p. 454.

[313] Sandys, J. E., *ibid.*

[314] *Ibid.*

[315] Jonas, *Vita Columbani*, p. 26, cited Sandys, *op. cit.* I., p. 456.

[316] Sandys, J. E., *ibid.*

[317] Hull, Eleanor, *Early Christian Ireland*, p. 274.

[318] Hull, Eleanor, *op. cit.* p. 276.

[319] Zimmer, H., *op. cit.* p. 116.

[320] Sandys, J. E., *History of Classical Scholarship*, I., p. 455; Zimmer, H., *Irish Element in Mediæval Culture*, p. 116; Hull, Eleanor, *Early Christian Ireland*, p. 276.

[321] See Stokes and Strachan, *Thesaurus Palaeohibernicus*, I., pp. xiii.–xxiv., II., pp. ix.–xxv.

[322] Joyce, P. W., *Social History of Ireland*, I., pp. 430–436.

[323] Rashdall, *Universities of Europe*, I., p. 36.

[324] Leach, A. F., *The Schools of Mediæval England*, p. 48.

[325] Healy, John, *op. cit.* pp. 202–204; Joyce, P. W., *op. cit.* I., p. 432.

[326] Sigerson, George, *Bards of the Gael and Gall*, p. 45.

[327] See above Chapter III.

[328] Healy, John, *op. cit.* 120–123.

[329] Stokes and Strachan, *Thesaurus Palaeohibernicus*, I., pp. 1–482.

[330] Migne, *Patrologia Latina*, Tomus 80, p. 328.

[331] Bede, *Historia Ecclesiastica Gentis Anglorum*, Liber III., Ch. 7.

[332] Roger, *L'Enseignement des Lettres Classiques*, p. 275.

[333] Bede, *op. cit.* III., 4.

[334] Roger, *op. cit.* p. 228.

[335] Roger, *ibid.*

[336] See *Note 41 above.*

[337] Healy, John, *op. cit.* p. 207.

[338] Migne, *Pat. Lat.*, Tomus 87.

[339] Healy, John, *op. cit.* pp. 236–239; Stokes, G., *R.I.A.*; May, 1892, p. 125.

[340] Ed. Stokes, Whitley, in *Transactions of the Royal Irish Academy, MSS. Series*, Vol. L., p. 139.

[341] *Revue Celtique,* XIV., p. 226. For examples of glosses belonging to the seventh, eighth and ninth centuries see Stokes and Strachan's *Thesaurus Palaeohibernicus,* 2 vol.

[342] Stokes and Strachan, *op. cit.* II., pp. xxiii., 415.

[343] Thurneysen, *Revue Celtique,* VI., pp. 336–347.

[344] Zimmer, H., *op. cit.* p. 62, cf. Dümmler in *Neues Archiv,* VI., 258. *Cruindmeli sive Fulcharii Ars Metrica.,* Vienna, 1883.

[345] Zimmer, H., *op. cit.* p. 63.

[346] *Op. cit.* p. 50.

[347] Published, Keil. *Grammatici Latini,* Leipsig, 1857, I., p. xix.

[348] *Ibid.* Turner, Wm., *Catholic University Bulletin,* XIII., p. 392.

[349] Zimmer, H., *Irish Element in Mediæval Culture,* p. 60.

[350] Zimmer, H., *op. cit.* p. 61. Turner, Wm., *Catholic University Bulletin,* XIII., p. 149. See also Chapter VII.

[351] *Poetae Aevi Caroli,* III., p. 691. Ozanam, F., *Documents Inedits.*

[352] Roger, M., *L'Enseignement des Lettres Classiques,* p. 229.

[353] Roger, M., *op. cit.* p. 262; Healy, John, *op. cit.* p. 237.

[354] Stokes and Strachan, *op. cit.* I., p. xxiii., II., p. xvii., pp. 46–48; Thurneysen, *Zeitschrift für Celtische Philologie,* III., p. 52, *seq.*

[355] Reeves, Wm., *Adamnan,* pp. 14, 140, 192, 229.

[356] Roger, M., *op. cit.* p. 262.

[357] Roger, M., *op. cit.* pp. 262–3, footnotes.

[358] Stokes and Strachan, *op. cit.* II., p. xiv.; Stokes, Whitley, *Tripartite Life of St. Patrick,* II., p. 269; Roger, M., *l.c.* p. 266.

[359] Chap. III.

[360] *Studies* (Dublin), September, 1918, for an article by Aubrey Gwynn arguing that St. Columban was thirty years old when he left Bangor. We, however, have accepted the (tentative) chronology of Helen Concannon whose *Life of St. Columban* is the best that has been published.

[361] De Jubainville, H. d'Arbois, *Littérature Celtique,* I., p. 373.

[362] De Jubainville, *op. cit.* I., pp. 373–375; Sigerson, *op. cit.* p. 407.

[363] Gundlach, *Mon. Ger. Epistolae*, III., Notes on *Epistolae Columbani*.

[364] Esposito, Mario, Articles *Hiberno-Latin MSS. in Belgian Libraries*, Art. in *Archivium Hibernicum*, III., p. 2; *The Latin Writers of Mediæval Ireland*, Art. in Hermathena, XIV., No. 33, pp. 519–529; Art. in *Irish Theological Quarterly*, IV., pp. 181–185.

[365] Published under the title *Peronna Scottorum* in *Sitzungsberichte* of the Academy of Munich, 1900, p. 490.

[366] Migne, *Pat. Lat.*, Tomus, 89, col. 96; *Epistolae Mer. et Karl Aevi*.

[367] Roger, M., *op. cit.* p. 260.

[368] Nolan, Thomas P., *Irish Universities and Culture*, p. 13.

[369] Ker, W. P., *The Dark Ages*, p. 319.

[370] Jonas, *Vita Columbani* in Krusch *Script. rer. Merov.*, IV., p. 71; cited by Roger, *op. cit.* p. 411.

[371] Roger, M., *op. cit.* p. 412.

[372] Turner, Wm., Article *Irish Teachers in the Carolingian Revival* in *Catholic University Bulletin*, XIII., p. 387.

[373] Turner, Wm., *op. cit.* XIII., p. 389. This article by Turner in the *Catholic University Bulletin*, XIII., pp. 283 *seq.* and 567 *seq.* is by far the most helpful contribution to the study of the Carolingian Revival. A valuable array of facts is given and the sources for further inquiry are pointed out.

[374] Manitius, Max, *Geschichte der Lateinischen Literatur des Mittelalters*, Teil I., München, 1911; Roger, M., *op. cit.* 1905; Esposito, Mario, *Knowledge of Greek in Ireland during the Middle Ages*, Article in *Studies*, Dublin, 1912.

[375] Quoted by Traube in *O Roma Nobilis*, p. 58; see Migne, *Pat. Lat.*, Tomus, 124, col. 1133d; De Jubainville, *op. cit.* I., p. 379.

[376] Roger takes this view *op. cit.* p. 229; cf. Gougaud, Dom. *Les Chrétientés Celtiques*, p. 251.

[377] *Amra Coluim Cille* in the *Irish Liber Hymnorum*, edited by Bernard and Atkinson, I., 162–183, II., 50–80, 223–35.

[378] Meyer, Kuno, *Learning in Ireland*, p. 26.

[379] Reeves, Wm., *Adamnan*, p. 158.

[380] Reeves, Wm., *ibid.*

[381] *Sitzungsberichte* of the Royal Academy of Berlin, 1909, p. 561.

[382] Meyer, Kuno, *op. cit.* p. 27.

[383] Note in a Würzburg MS. of eighth century quoted by Zimmer in *Pelagius in Ireland*, p. 5.

[384] Keller, F., *Bilder und Schriftzugein den irischen Manuscripten in Mitteilungen des antiquarischen Gesellschaft in Zurich*, II., 61.

[385] Reeves, Wm., *Adamnan*, pp. xiv., xv., xxi. and Plates I., II., III.

[386] Stokes and Strachan, *Thesaurus Palaeohibernicus*, II., p. xiv.

[387] Stokes and Strachan, *op. cit.* II., pp. 159, 158, 169.

[388] See Giles, *Aldhelmi Opera*, p. 94.

[389] Bede, *op. cit.* Liber IV., Ch. I.

[390] Ed. Stokes, Whitley, *Three Irish Glosses*, London, 1862.

[391] In *Duil Dromma Ceta* (Egerton MS. 1782 15a ff; h. 3, 1863, ff T.C.D., 1317).

[392] Hyde, Douglas, *Literary History of Ireland*, p. 420.

[393] The celebrated *Vocabularius S. Galli* written in 780 A.D. in the Irish style of writing containing some of the earliest examples of German and French is believed to be the work of an Irish monk. See Zimmer, H., *Irish Element*, p. 71.

[394] Zimmer, H., *op. cit.* p. 68.

[395] Sandys, J. E., *History of Classical Scholarship*, I., p. 463.

[396] Meyer, Kuno, *Triads of Ireland*, p. xiv.

[397] *Monumenta Germaniae Historiae*, Epistolae, III., p. 318.

[398] Flood, J. M., *Ireland: Its Saints and Scholars*, p. 92.

[399] Traube, L., *O Roma Nobilis*, p. 61.

[400] *Ibid.*

[401] Zimmer, *op. cit.* p. 126.

[402] For further details see Traube, L., *O Roma Nobilis*, p. 61. Also Norden, *Die Antike Kunstprosa*, p. 666, Note 1.

[403] De Jubainville, H. d'Arbois, *op. cit.* I., p. 397.

[404] Traube, L., *O Roma Nobilis*, p. 287.

[405] Of the non-Irish of the time only Eric of Auxerre, Christian of Stavelot, and Walafrid knew Greek, Traube, *op. cit.* p. 65.

[406] Concannon, Helen, *Life of St. Columban*, p. 287.

[407] Michelet, *Histoire de France*, I., p. 121.

[408] Healy, John, Art. in *Irish Ecclesiastical Record*, 1880, p. 16.

[409] Mullinger, H. B., *The Schools of Charles the Great*, p. 118.

[410] Newman, John H., *Idea of a University*, p. 485.

[411] Renan, E., in *Sur l'Étude de la langue grecque au Moyen Age*, cited by Flood, J. M. in *Ireland: its Saints and Scholars*, p. 7.

[412] Baluze, *Miscellanea*, V., p. 54, cited by Mullinger, *op. cit.* p. 119.

[413] Mullinger, *op. cit.* p. 119.

[414] Mullinger, *ibid.*

[415] Flood, W. H. Grattan, *History of Irish Music*, p. 4.

[416] Joyce, P. W., *op. cit.* I., p. 571.

[417] O'Curry, Eugene, *Manners and Customs of the Ancient Irish.*

[418] Joyce, P. W., *Social History of Ireland.*

[419] Flood, W. H. Grattan, *History of Irish Music.*

[420] Flood, W. H. Grattan, *op. cit.* p. 20.

[421] Joyce, P. W., *op. cit.* I.; Flood, W. H., *op. cit.* p. 10.

[422] Quoted in *Irish Ecclesiastical Record*, 1883, p. 510.

[423] Keller, F., *Ulster Journal of Archæology*, VIII., p. 218.

[424] Joyce, P. W., *op. cit.* I., p. 572.

[425] Wood-Martin, W. G., *Pagan Ireland*, illustrations; Joyce, *op. cit.* I., 675, 582.

[426] Joyce, P. W., *op. cit.* I., pp. 576, 582.

[427] Bollandists, *Acta Sanctorum*, p. 595; Lanigan, *Ecclesiastical History of Ireland*, II., p. 464; Joyce, *op. cit.* I., p. 572.

[428] Flood, W. H. G., *op. cit.* pp. 7, 8.

[429] Flood, W. H. G., *op. cit.* p. 12.

[430] Zimmer, H., *op. cit.* p. 73.

[431] Zimmer, H., *ibid.*

[432] Matthew, *History of Music*, cited by Flood, *op. cit.* p. 15.

[433] Zimmer, H., *op. cit.* p. 76.

[434] Zimmer, H., *op. cit.* p. 77.

[435] Flood, W. H. G., *op. cit.* p. 15.

[436] Flood, W. H. G., Article *Irish Music in Glories of Ireland*, p. 71.

[437] Schubiger, *Die Sängerschule St. Gallen*, p. 33; Flood, W. H. G., *History of Irish Music*, pp. 16–19; Joyce, P. W., *op. cit.* I., 573.

[438] Flood, W. H. G., Article *Irish Music* in *Glories of Ireland*, p. 771.

[439] See *Liber Hymnorum*, ed. by Atkinson and Bernard; also Stokes and Strachan, *Thesaurus Palaeohibernicus*, I., 298 *seq.*

[440] Flood, W. H. G., Art. in *Glories of Ireland*, p. 72.

[441] Turner, Wm., *History of Philosophy*, p. 247. (Query: Is this the same or a different commentary from that referred to by and attributed to Bishop Donnchadh, by Flood?)

[442] Flood, W. H. G., *History of Irish Music*, pp. 19, 20.

[443] See Coffey, George, *Bronze Age in Ireland*, Plates II., V., VII., VIII., IX., X. and pp. 48, 49, 50.

[444] McKenna, James E. (Right Rev.), *Irish Art*, p. 7.

[445] McKenna, James E., *op. cit.* pp. 8, 9.

[446] Sullivan, Sir Edward, *The Book of Kells,*, Introduction, p. 1.

[447] Westwood, John, *Palaeographia Sacra Pictoria*, quoted by McKenna, James E., *op. cit.* pp. 20–21.

[448] Coffey, George, *Guide to the Celtic Antiquities of Christian Ireland*, pp. 9, 10.

[449] Quoted by McKenna, James F., *op. cit.* p. 20, 21.

[450] Hartley, *Proceedings of the Royal Dublin Society*, N.S., IV., 1885.

[451] See *Ireland: Industrial and Agricultural*, pp. 19, 20 for the places where these materials are obtainable in Ireland.

[452] Joyce, P. W., *op. cit.* I., 561; Coffey, G., *Bronze Age.* Illustration.

[453] Stokes, Wm., *Life of Petrie,* Chap. vii.

[454] Joyce, P. W., *op. cit.* I., p. 561.

[455] Joyce, P. W., *op. cit.* I., pp. 560–563.

[456] Coffey, G., *Guide to Antiquities of Christian Ireland.* Illustration.

[457] Joyce, P. W., *op. cit.* I., p. 560.

[458] Joyce, P. W., *op. cit.* I., p. 567.

[459] MacAlister, R. A. S., *Muiredach, Abbot of Monasterboice* (890–923 A.D.). This work gives a detailed account of one of these crosses at Monasterboice.

[460] Abelson, Paul, *The Seven Liberal Arts*, p. 64.

[461] Text in Migne, *Latin Patrology*, Vol. 90, Col. 294–578.

[462] Text in Migne, *Latin Patrology*, Vol. 107, Col. 669–727.

[463] See Abelson, Paul, *op. cit.* p. 90.

[464] Abelson, Paul, *op. cit.* p. 100; Turner, Wm., *Hist. of Phil.*, p. 257.

[465] Abelson, Paul, *op. cit.* p. 104.

[466] Abelson, Paul, *op. cit.* pp. 103–104.

[467] Abelson, Paul, *op. cit.* pp. 113–114.

[468] *De Nuptiis*, etc., Eyssenhardt ed. pp. 194–254.

[469] Text in Migne, Vol. 70, c. 1212–1216.

[470] Text in Migne, Vol. 82, c. 161–163.

[471] *Dictionary of National Biography*, Vol. I., p. 93.

[472] Maguire, Eugene, *Life of Adamnan*, p. 95.

[473] Chap. V., p. 69, Text and translation in *Proceedings of the Royal Irish Academy*, 1883, pp. 219–252.

[474] See MacAlister, R. A. S., *Muiredach, Abbot of Clonmacnoise*, where a copy of this map will be found.

[475] See Mullinger, J. B., *The Schools of Charles the Great*, p. 120, for Alcuin's silly explanations of astronomical phenomena.

[476] The Vernacular Studies would naturally be confined chiefly to the schools situated in Ireland. It is possible that they were taught in some of the schools in Scotland and in those schools on the Continent which had Irish pupils. It might be remarked that some writers attribute the early literary development of vernacular poetry in Northern England to the example set by the Irish monks in using their native tongue for poetry.

[477] Perhaps Clement, the successor of Alcuin at the Palace School, should also be ranked as one of the greatest Irish scholars. It is well known that he was a famous Greek scholar and is believed by many to have been a much greater scholar than Alcuin, his rival in royal favour. We have not yet

succeeded in collecting sufficient evidence to warrant his inclusion in the present connection.

[478] Lecky, *Rationalism in Europe*, III., p. 5.

[479] Zimmer, H., *Irish Element*, p. 62; Healy, John, *op. cit.* p. 369.

[480] Healy, John, *op. cit.* pp. 569–571.

[481] Healy, John, *op. cit.* p. 571.

[482] Zimmer, H., *Irish Element*, pp. 62–63.

[483] *Annals of the Four Masters*, I., sub anno 784 A.D.

[484] Published by Walckenaer, Paris, 1807; by Letronne in a more critical edition, Paris, 1814; by Gustav Parthey, Berlin, 1870.

[485] *Dictionary of National Biography*, XV., pp. 48–49.

[486] Healy, John, *op. cit.* p. 283.

[487] *Dictionary of National Biography*, Vol. XV., pp. 49–50.

[488] Zimmer, H., *Irish Element in Mediæval Culture*, pp. 55–56.

[489] Turner, Wm., *Catholic University Bulletin*, Vol. XIII., p. 396.

[490] Turner, Wm. *op. cit.* p. 396.

[491] *Poetae Aevi Carolini*, III., p. 691.

[492] In the *Valenciennes Codex*, 386, pp. 73–76, cited by Turner, *ibid.*

[493] Turner, Wm., *op. cit.* p. 395.

[494] Migne, *Pat. Lat.*, Tom. 105, p. 477.

[495] Healy, John, *op. cit.* p. 383.

[496] Turner, W., *op. cit.* p. 392.

[497] Pertz, *Monumenta Germaniae Historica*, Leg. I., p. 249. Stokes, Margaret, *Six Months in the Appenines*, App. VIII., p. 205. Muratori, *Antiquitates Italicae*, Tom. III., Dissertatio, 43.

[498] Stokes, Margaret, *ibid.*

[499] *Poetae Caroli*, I., pp. 396, 408, 411, 413, 429, 430, 511.

[500] Healy, John, *op. cit.* p. 392.

[501] Zimmer, H., *op. cit.* p. 11.

[502] Entitled *Dungali Responsa contra Perversae Claudii Taurinensis Episcopi Sententias*.

[503] Cited by Lanigan in *Ecclesiastical History of Ireland*, III., Chap. XX.

[504] Healy, John, *op. cit.* p. 391.

[505] Stokes, Margaret, *Six Months in the Appenines*, p. 213.

[506] For list see Miss Stokes, *op. cit.* pp. 296–297.

[507] Muratori, *Antiquitates Italicae*, Dissert. Tom. iii., col. 821.

[508] See Stokes, Margaret, *op. cit.* p. 216 for contents.

[509] About 90 of his poems are published by Traube, *Poetae Aev. Carl.*

[510] See his tract *Artem Euticii Grammatici* in Traube's *O Roma Nobilis*, p. 61, which shows a knowledge of Greek. Traube thinks it was composed in Ireland.

[511] Montfaucon, *Pal. Graeca*, p. 235, describes the Greek Psalter transcribed by Sedulius now No. 8047 in the Library at the Arsenale at Paris.

[512] First published by Cardinal Mai in *Specilegium Romanus*; also by Traube in *Quellen u. Untersuchungen zur lateinischen Philologie des Mittelalters*; Teil I., Erstes Heft von S. Hellman, München, 1906, pp. 203, Zweites Heft Johannes Scottus von Edward Kennard Rand, München, 1906, p. 106.

[513] Turner, Book Review in *Cath. Univ. Bulletin*, xiii., p. 149.

[514] *Ibid.*

[515] Traube, *O Roma Nobilis*; Turner, Wm., *op. cit.* p. 397.

[516] Baemker in *Jahrbuch für Philosophie und Spekulative Theologie*, Band VII., p. 346, Bd. VIII., p. 222; Healy, John, *op. cit.* p. 578.

[517] De Wülf, M., *History of Mediæval Philosophy*, p. 246.

[518] The Council of Eperny (846 A.D.) speaks of *Hospitalia Scottorum*, "quae sancti homines illius gentis in hoc regno construxerunt"; *Mon. Ger. Leg.* I., 390; Warren, F. E., *op. cit.* p. 15.

[519] Many believe that Eriugena was a layman.

[520] Flood, F. M., *Ireland: its Schools and Scholars*, pp. 94–95.

[521] Flood, F. M., *op. cit.* p. 95, where the above is quoted.

[522] Text of Eriugena's works in Migne, *Pat. Lat.*, Tom. 122, with Preface by Gale and Schulter.

[523] In the Library of the British Museum, Harleian, 2506; Turner, Wm., Art. *Irish Teachers in the Carolingian Revival*, *op. cit.* XIII., 256.

[524] Mullinger, J. B., *op. cit.* p. 171.

[525] De Wülf, Maurice, *History of Mediæval Philosophy*, English translation by Dr. P. Coffey, p. 167.

[526] Turner, Wm., *History of Philosophy*, p. 257.

[527] De Wülf, M., *op. cit.* pp. 167–168.

[528] Turner, Wm., *op. cit.* p. 256.

[529] Migne, *Pat. Lat.* Tom. 122, *De Predestinatione*, I., 1.

[530] Erdman, *History of Philosophy*, English translation by Williston S. Hough, Vol. I., p. 292.

[531] *De Divisione Naturae*, I., p. 69.

[532] *Ibid.*, IV.

[533] Turner, Wm., *loc. cit.* p. 249.

[534] *Ibid.*

[535] Poole, Reginald Lane, *Illustration in the History of Mediæval Thought.* See *Excurus on Visit to Greece*, Legend Examined, pp. 311–313.

[536] For numerous complimentary tributes see T. P. Nolan's booklet *Irish University and Culture* in the Catholic Truth Society Series.

[537] Poole, Reginald Lane, *op. cit.* p. 14.

[538] Turner, Wm., Article *Irish Teachers in the Carolingian Revival* in *Catholic University Bulletin*, Vol. XIII., pp. 579–580.

[539] Zimmer H., *The Irish Element in Mediæval Culture*, p. 130.